CREATIVE
Sugar Art
DESIGN

BERNICE VERCOE

GOLDEN PRESS

Dedication

I dedicate this book to my grandchildren,
Glen, Ray, Kate, Carly, Krystal, Mitchell and Hayden,
with all my love.

First published 1990 by
Golden Press Pty Ltd, Incorporated in NSW
46 Egerton Street, Silverwater NSW 2141, Australia
717 Rosebank Road, Avondale, Auckland, New Zealand

National Library of Australia Cataloguing-in-publication data

Vercoe, Bernice J. (Bernice Jean)
Creative sugar art design

ISBN 0 7302 0115 5

1. Sugar art. 2. Cake decorating. I. Title

641.6'36

Photography: David Levin Studios, North Sydney
Editor: Susan Tomnay
Printing arranged by Imago Productions (F.E.) Pte Ltd, Singapore

CONTENTS

FOREWORD

Writing this foreword for Bernice Vercoe's new book *Creative Sugar Art Design* is a great honour and real pleasure.

I believe that through her teaching and her books, Mrs Vercoe has done more than any other individual to promote cake decorating and sugar art.

Her first book *Cake Design and Decorating* was first published in 1966. This was followed, in 1974 by two more books *Australian Book of Cake Decorating* and *Discovering Cake Decorating*.

Many of the top decorators in the world learned this fascinating art from these books. It is no small wonder that the interest in cake decorating has grown unbelievably during the past fifteen years.

Cake decorators in many countries have looked forward to another book from the pen of this very talented sugar artist and daughter of Australia. We are therefore delighted to welcome *Creative Sugar Art Design* into our midst. It covers many special techniques, a large variety of hand-moulded flowers, foliage, cakes for special occasions, sugar art objects and advice to the exhibitor from the judge. Every aspect is clearly explained.

Mrs Vercoe is well qualified and has considerable experience. She is a fully trained teacher, taught classes for the Education Department and later T.A.F.E. (Technical and Further Education) for thirty-six years. She retired as Head Teacher in Home Science in 1984, but is still very much involved with all facets of this work.

In 1973 she was invited to teach the Australian method of cake decorating in the U.S.A. and in 1979 received a further invitation to judge and demonstrate in South Africa. In the same year she founded the Cake Decorators' Guild of NSW.

The International Cake Exploration Society of U.S.A., in 1981, placed her name in the Society's Hall of Fame.

She took an exhibition of sugar work to the 1982 Trade Fair at Guangzhou, China, sponsored by the NSW Government, where she demonstrated the technique of sugar flower making.

She was responsible for showing the first exhibition of decorated cakes and sugar work at art level in NSW Galleries.

In 1986 came a second invitation to judge and demonstrate in Zimbabwe and South Africa.

Over the years Mrs Vercoe has been one of Australia's top judges and a leading authority on cake decorating. She has also encouraged the spread of knowledge and techniques from other countries in her homeland. She has been a prolific winner of show awards throughout her career.

On behalf of the ever increasing number of cake decorators all over the world, I want to thank Bernice Vercoe for her dedication and inspiration and for sharing with all of us her knowledge acquired through considerable experience over so many years.

I am certain that all cake decorators will benefit greatly by this book.

Gladiola Botha

Gladiola Botha
Past President
Cake Decorators' Guild
of South Africa.

page 6

Patchwork applique in sugar paste. This beautiful card is a most effective way of saying "Happy Birthday," to someone you love (see page 124).

INTRODUCTION

This book should assist both the novice and the advanced decorator furthering their achievements in the skilled techniques of cake decorating and sugar art.

Although I have written three books on this subject, I have repeated some of the basic instructions in this book, so that the beginner will be aware of the terminology and techniques applied in the craft.

I will not presume to say at which stage the beginner becomes advanced, but rather leave that decision to the individual to determine his or her capabilities and to know when to attempt the various challenges offered.

The purpose of this book is to cover the basics of cake decorating, to update creations in design, to describe specific skills recently introduced by Australian and overseas decorators and to provide a suitable textbook for both teacher and pupil.

Cake decorating and sugar art gives pleasure to so many. It is a means whereby the decorator may pursue individual creative desires for personal enjoyment and satisfaction. It holds no limit to age and can be as rewarding to the older person as to the young.

My hope is that this book will bring many hours of enjoyment and fulfilment to all who are interested in this fascinating field.

Bernice J. Vercoe

ACKNOWLEDGEMENTS

I wish to express my gratitude and acknowledgement to some very talented decorators who so kindly allowed their beautiful work to form part of this book:

Lyn Coltman, Forestville, NSW; Mary Lynas, Seaforth, NSW; Mavis Mepham, Lambton, NSW; Gill Hogg (formerly Heinrich), Naracoorte, SA; Jeanette van Niekirk, Kempton Park, South Africa; Colleen Willis, Marlborough, Zimbabwe.

To my dear friend Gladiola Botha, the first and now the past President of the Cake Decorators' Guild of South Africa, for her faith in my ability and for writing such a wonderful foreword for this book.

To my husband Raymond Vercoe, for his valuable assistance during my planning and preparation of typescripts and his patience and support throughout my many years as an addicted cake decorator.

Offray
DESIGNER
RIBBONS
Offray
DESIGNER
RIBBONS
RIBBONS

MATERIALS & EQUIPMENT

It is wise for the beginner to purchase the minimum amount of equipment and add extras to it as experience is gained and the love of this art develops.

Numerous sizes and types of tubes are used for pipework. These should be of top quality and made from a non-corrosive metal to give high performance and many years' service.

Tubes and other decorating requirements may be purchased from cake decorating supply shops and specialty shops.

Tubes recommended as a basic kit

Writing tubes	Nos	00, 0, 1, 2, 3
Petal tubes		20 medium and small
Shell or Star tubes		5, 8
Half Shell tube		35
Basket tube		22
Leaf tube		17

All tubes listed may be used by both left and right-handed decorators with the exception of petal tube No. 20, used for piped flower work. This is available with both left-sloping and right-sloping tubes.

Tube numbers may vary in some countries. As the decorator becomes more proficient, finer writing tubes such as the No. 0000 and 000 may be added to the basic list.

Care should be taken to soak the tubes in hot water after use and to clean them with a soft hair paintbrush or a special brush for this purpose. Do not use sharp pointed metal objects as these will cause damage to the tubes and affect their performance. Rinse the tubes well in clean water and dry carefully before putting them away.

Other accessories for the decorator

Scissors

Both large and small scissors are necessary. Use the larger pair for cutting patterns, paper, ribbon and accessories. Use the small, thin-bladed, pointed surgical or embroidery scissors for fine cutting when moulding flowers and foliage.

Wire

Special covered wire is used in cake decorating.
0.008 inch fine wire for small flowers and leaves.
0.0148 inch medium wire for medium flowers.
0.018 inch heavy wire for larger flowers.

Wire cutters

These should be of good quality to enable you to cleanly cut wire into lengths suitable for flowers and sprays.

Florist wire

Nos. 18, 22, 24.
Suitable to extend stem lengths for spray work.

Florist tape

For covering florist wire and taping wires used in moulded flower and leaf work. Available in brown, white and green.

Stamens

Available in all colours. It is economical to purchase white stamens and tint them to suit the flower. Stamens are made with fine, medium and coarse tips. The fine tips look more delicate in most flowers.

Tweezers

A pair of long, pointed, surgical tweezers are essential for floral arrangements. A cheaper pair of short tweezers with flat tops are also very useful.

Ribbon

Choice of width depends on the needs of the decorator. The most popular sizes are 1.5 mm, 3 mm and 5 mm. Satin ribbon is used most often.

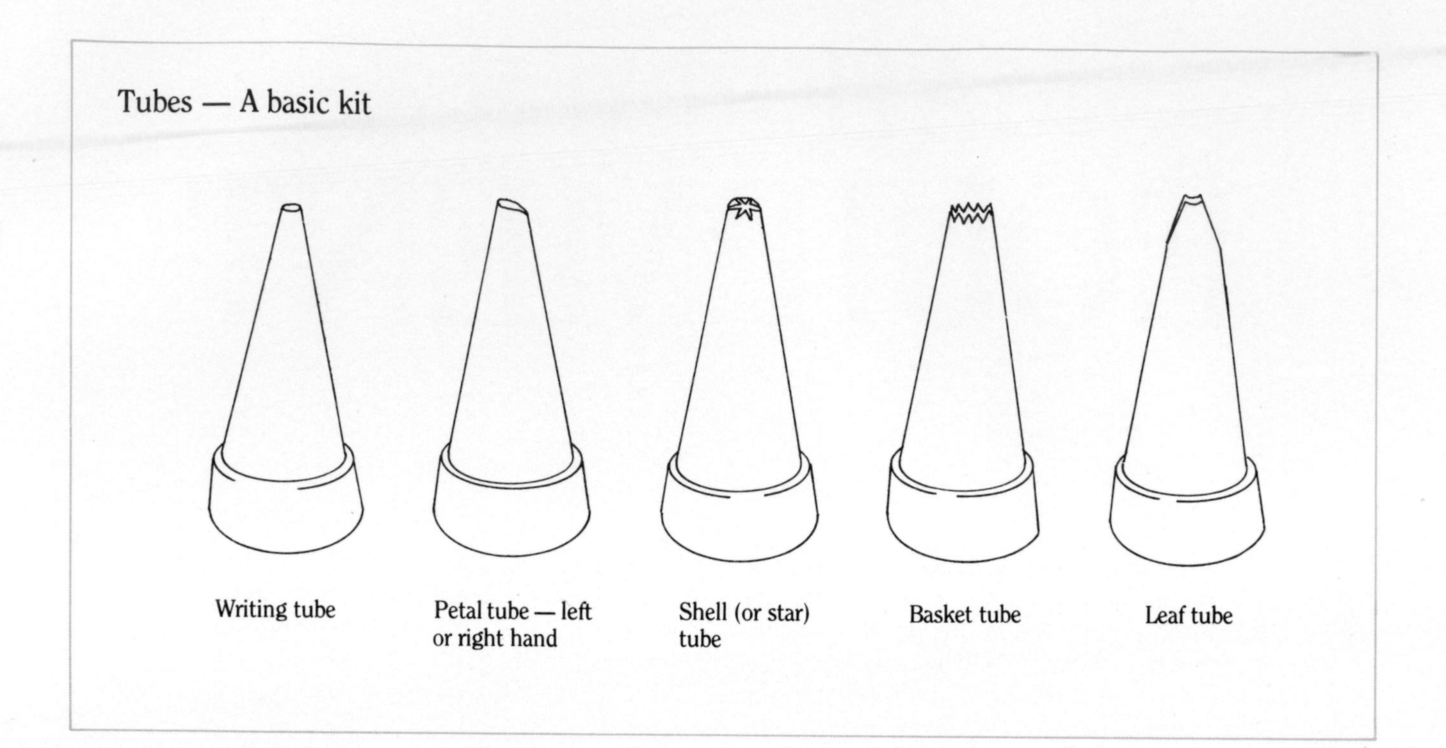

Offray double sided satin ribbon has been used throughout this book.

Flower cutters

Many shapes and sizes in both metal and plastic are available for the decorator's needs.

Special tools

Tools are available for balling, marking and frilling. They are sold in sets or separately.

Cake smoothers

These help give a smoother and more even surface to the rolled fondant after covering the cake.

Turntable

Depending on the decorator's needs, a turntable may be a simple and homemade one, or a commercially-made turntable which may have other advantages such as tilting and height adjustment.

Cake boards

These should suit the shape of the cake. Strong boards are essential; they should be sufficiently rigid to take the weight of a heavy cake.

They should be wide enough to give protection when handling, whilst having regard to appearance and balance. Often the design and decoration dictate the minimum size of the board.

Board covering

Special papers are available from specialty shops for covering boards. Satin and other materials may also be used. Boards may also be covered with fondant or flood work and edged with a beading.

Food colouring

Edible food colouring is available in liquid, paste and powder form. It is essential to use quality products. When adding colours to royal icing, fondant or modelling paste, use restraint.

If using liquid colour, add it carefully with an eye dropper or skewer. To add paste colour, use a toothpick or skewer. When using powdered food colours, dissolve a small amount of the powder in a little hot water, mix well to dissolve the grains and add to the mixture as recommended for liquid colour.

Non-toxic powdered chalk is used for dusting. It is applied in its dry state with the aid of a soft-haired paintbrush. It should be noted that non-toxic chalk is a completely different medium to edible powdered food colouring which is dissolved and added to royal icing, fondant and modelling paste. Chalk or petal dust is applied as the final touch to give depth of colour to the finished moulded work or sugar art.

Piping bags

Piping bags may be made from materials such as jaconet, nylon or plastic. These are obtainable ready made. Paper cones may be made from strong greaseproof paper, parchment or cellophane. The cone method is a clean, hygienic and economical method of decorating.

Paper cone making for small bag

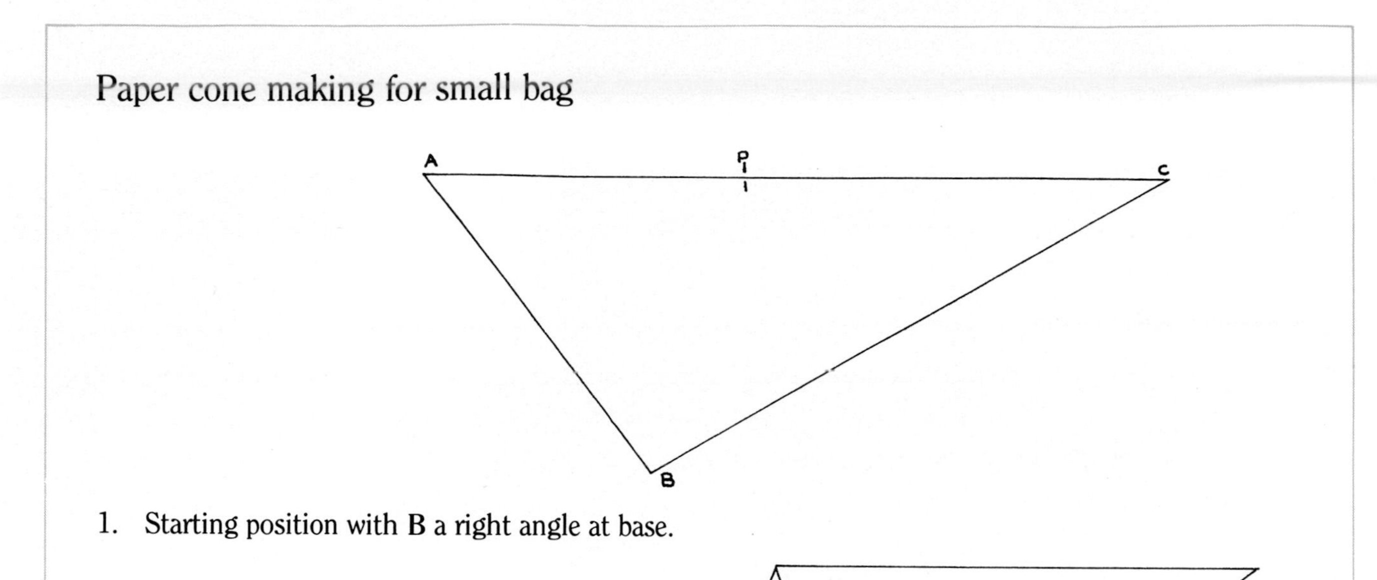

1. Starting position with **B** a right angle at base.

2. Turn corner **A** over towards you, fingers under, thumb on top, pointing in the direction of the arrow. *Do not* release this grip until the cone is almost completed.

3. By reversing the left hand to "thumb down" with the right hand holding and adjusting the tension at **C**, a cone can be formed with an apex **P** along the side **AC**.

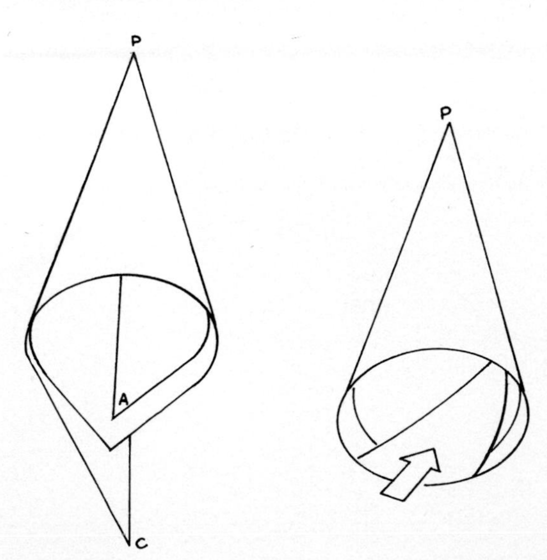

4. By maintaining a firm hold on **A** with the left hand, take corner **C** and wrap it twice around the cone, varying the direction and tension so as to achieve a sharp point at apex **P**, a slight parallel overlap at the edge of **PC** (outside).

See following page for dimensions of paper cones.

Paper cones

A sheet of greaseproof paper measuring approximately 45 cm x 33½ cm folded diagonally x 55 cm
45 cm x 31½ cm

A sheet cut as quoted yields 2 large bags

For the medium and large bags — cut a piece from the apex and insert the tube

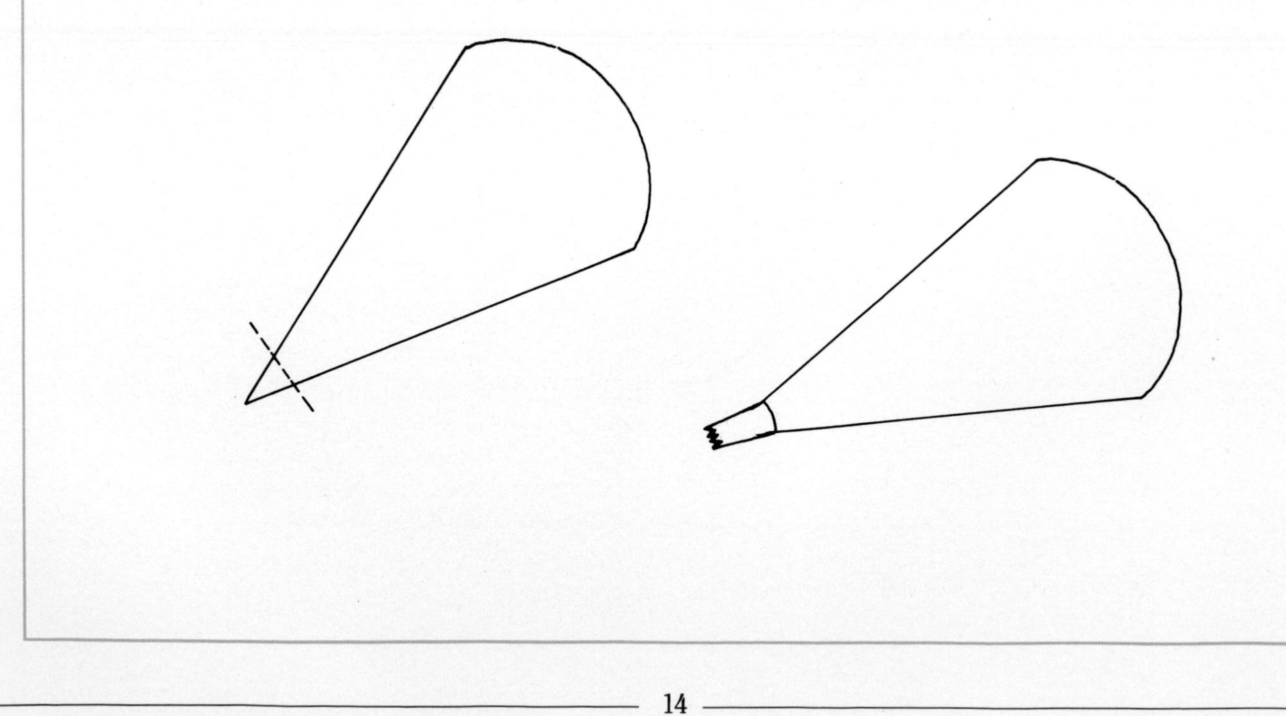

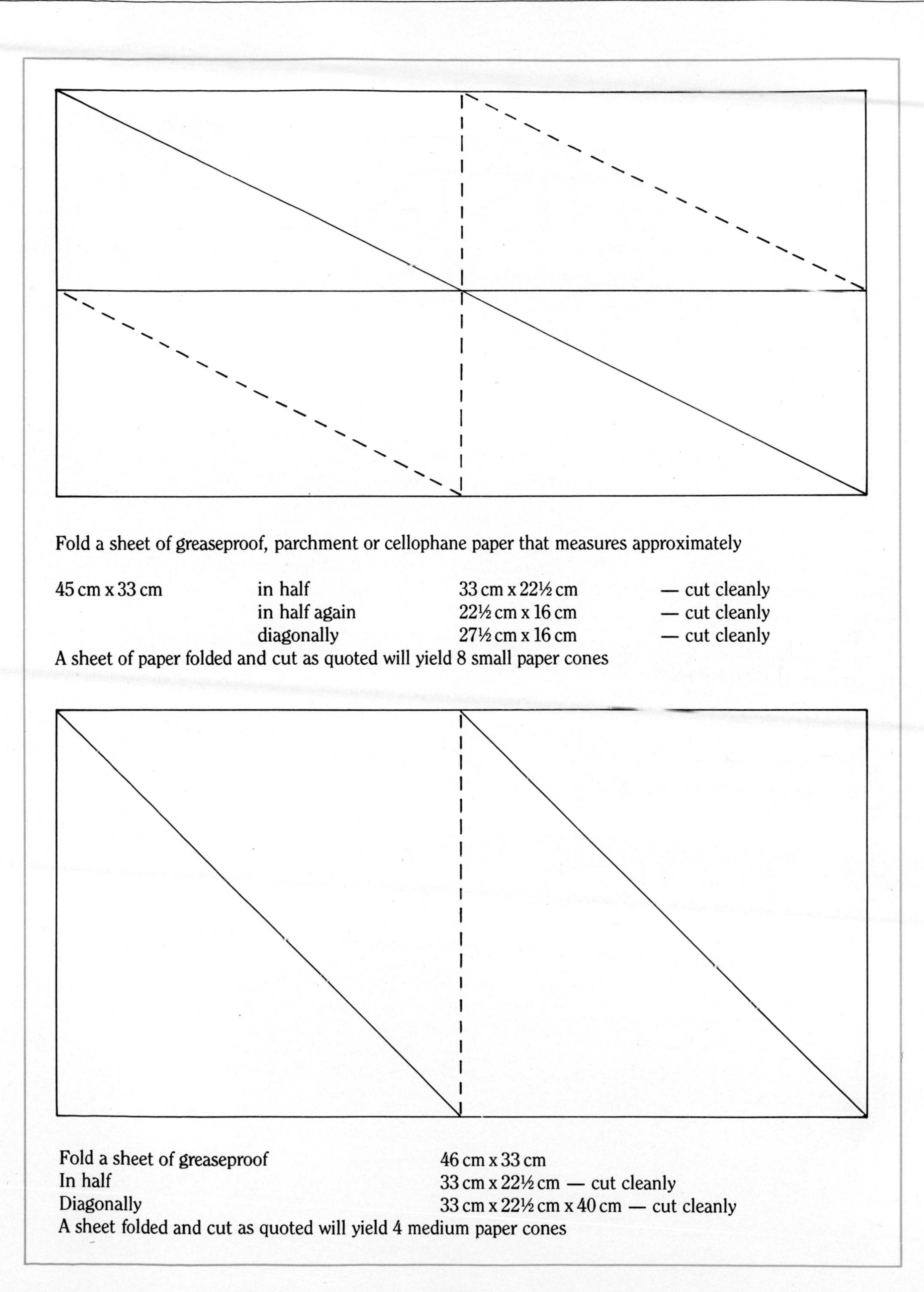

Fold a sheet of greaseproof, parchment or cellophane paper that measures approximately

45 cm x 33 cm	in half	33 cm x 22½ cm	— cut cleanly
	in half again	22½ cm x 16 cm	— cut cleanly
	diagonally	27½ cm x 16 cm	— cut cleanly

A sheet of paper folded and cut as quoted will yield 8 small paper cones

Fold a sheet of greaseproof	46 cm x 33 cm
In half	33 cm x 22½ cm — cut cleanly
Diagonally	33 cm x 22½ cm x 40 cm — cut cleanly

A sheet folded and cut as quoted will yield 4 medium paper cones

ROYAL ICING & ITS USES

Royal icing

Royal icing is used for pipework with all sized tubes, from the finest to the largest. It is also broken down with water and used for flooded motifs or run-in sugar work, (see page 26).

Unless the correct consistency is achieved in the mixing, difficulties may occur, especially when using the finer tubes. It is only after preparing several batches of this mixture that the novice will gain the necessary judgment and skill to produce a satisfactory working medium with the appropriate consistency. Achievement of success in this regard is of utmost importance and experience is the ultimate teacher.

The following points must be observed:

1. The egg white used must be fresh and at room temperature.
2. The icing sugar *must* be pure and finely sifted.
3. When adding the sugar gradually to the egg white, it is always wise to beat each addition very well, particularly in the early stages. A steady circular movement with a wooden spoon or metal spatula is the best method of beating; it is not good enough just to stir.
4. A drop or two of acetic acid will give cohesion to the egg white and produce a lightness to the royal icing. But over-use of this acid will cause drying and produce a brittle mixture when piping. When adding it to the mixture, use an eyedropper.

Testing Royal Icing consistency

Royal icing recipe

1 egg white, at room temperature
350 g pure icing sugar, sifted (the amount of sugar will vary with the size of the egg)
1 or 2 drops of acetic acid, 60% strength (this is obtainable from the chemist)

1. Place the egg white in a small glass or crockery mixing bowl. Make sure the bowl and equipment for use have been washed and dried and are perfectly clean, to ensure an optimum result.
2. Add 2 rounded tablespoons icing sugar and beat well until it has thoroughly combined with the egg white. This will take 2-3 minutes of hand beating.
3. Continue to add the sugar, reducing it now to 1 tablespoon at a time. Beat well between each addition until the mixture resembles a syrup consistency and maintains a smoothness and gloss throughout the beating.
4. Add 1 or 2 drops of acetic acid. Continue to add icing sugar 1 teaspoon at a time, beating well between each addition, until the mixture reaches a "soft peak" or "lattice" consistency.

This stage is reached when the royal icing peaks on the back of a spoon. When the spoon is reversed, the peak will stand erect, then tilt to a 45° angle. This consistency is used for writing, dots, lattice, embroidery, tulle work, bridgework (drop lines) and lace.

The "firm peak" stage is achieved by beating a little extra sugar into the mixture. The peak should stand smooth, tapered and erect on the back of the spoon. This consistency is used for shell border work, piped flowers and leaves.

Note: Decorators who have "hot" hands may need to alter these guideline stages to suit themselves.

Soft peak consistency royal icing was used for embroidery, lace and pleated extension on this beautiful cake. (See illustration on page 43)

To fill the icing bag

Small paper cone

1. First form a circle with the thumb and index finger of the left hand (or right hand, if left handed).
2. Place the bag, point first, through the circle until the shape of the cone fits comfortably to the hole formed by the fingers. The flap of the bag, C, which has been tucked into the cone to secure the bag, should be placed topside to the index finger and not resting on the thumb.
3. Using a small spatula or a knife take a small amount of royal icing from the container or bowl, insert the blade into the paper cone with the icing facing downward towards the thumb. Use the thumb as a pressure point to wipe the icing from the knife and into the bag.
4. Repeat this process until the bag is half to three-quarters full before removing the cone from the finger circle.
5. To fold the bag, turn a fold approximately 1 cm wide from the right hand topside towards the centre, then another the same width from the left hand side towards the centre. Then fold the remaining peak of the bag over to the front and continue folding until the icing is firmly enclosed within a well-sealed piping bag which should remain firm and compact throughout its use. To accomplish this, it is necessary to continually "fold in" as required.

Positioning the bag for use

The small bag is held in a similar way as a pen or pencil for writing. The difference is that the thumb is lifted from the side of the bag and placed directly to the top. The thumb is the main pressure control used to force the royal icing through the aperture cut in the point.

Note: A well-made bag should have a sharp clean point from which no icing flows until just prior to use when the point is cut to size with a pair of scissors.

Tubes are more successfully used in the medium and large bags whereas the small cone is very efficient for fine to medium pipework or it can produce an excellent royal icing leaf by flattening the point of the filled bag between the fingers and cutting a small, even-mitred point.

Medium and large bags

1. Before filling the bags with royal icing, cut sufficient from the pointed tip to allow approximately 1/3rd of the tube to protrude, once inserted inside the bag.
2. Hold the paper cone, gently yet firmly in the left hand (or if left handed, right hand). Lift a scoop of royal icing from the bowl with a wooden spoon or spatula and shake it into the open bag.
3. Repeat this process until the bag is half full. Fold both sides of the top of the bag in towards the centre as previously described for the small cone and fold the top peak of the bag over the front, enclosing the royal icing. Continue to fold and tuck until the icing is well sealed within and ready for use.
4. The bag should remain firmly compact throughout its use by continuous "folding in".

Positioning the bag for use

1. Fully open the hand and lay the bag diagonally across the palm with the tube end extending beyond the small finger. The top should fit snugly under the thumb.
2. Close the hand by wrapping the four fingers around the bag, then lower the thumb over the top folded position of the bag and gently squeeze until the icing flows from the tube.
3. When not in use, place the tube end under a damp cloth or stand erect in a tumbler on a damp sponge. See page 114 hint 5.

Royal icing for oriental stringwork

This icing is recommended by Geraldine Randlesome, a talented cake decorator from Canada. It is excellent for oriental stringwork because of its capacity to stretch.

1 egg white
300 g approximately pure sifted icing sugar
⅛ teaspoon gum arabic
¼ teaspoon liquid glucose

1. Place the egg white in a glass bowl.
2. Add the icing sugar a teaspoon at a time, mixing well between each addition. Continue beating until the mixture forms a soft peak.
3. Sift in the gum arabic and beat well. Continue to beat until a stiff peak is reached, then add the glucose and mix well.
4. Place the icing into a clean container. Cover with plastic cling wrap and a lid before storing.

Freehand embroidered patterns

These are suitable for special occasion cakes. Royal icing used in executing this work should be of a "soft peak" consistency.

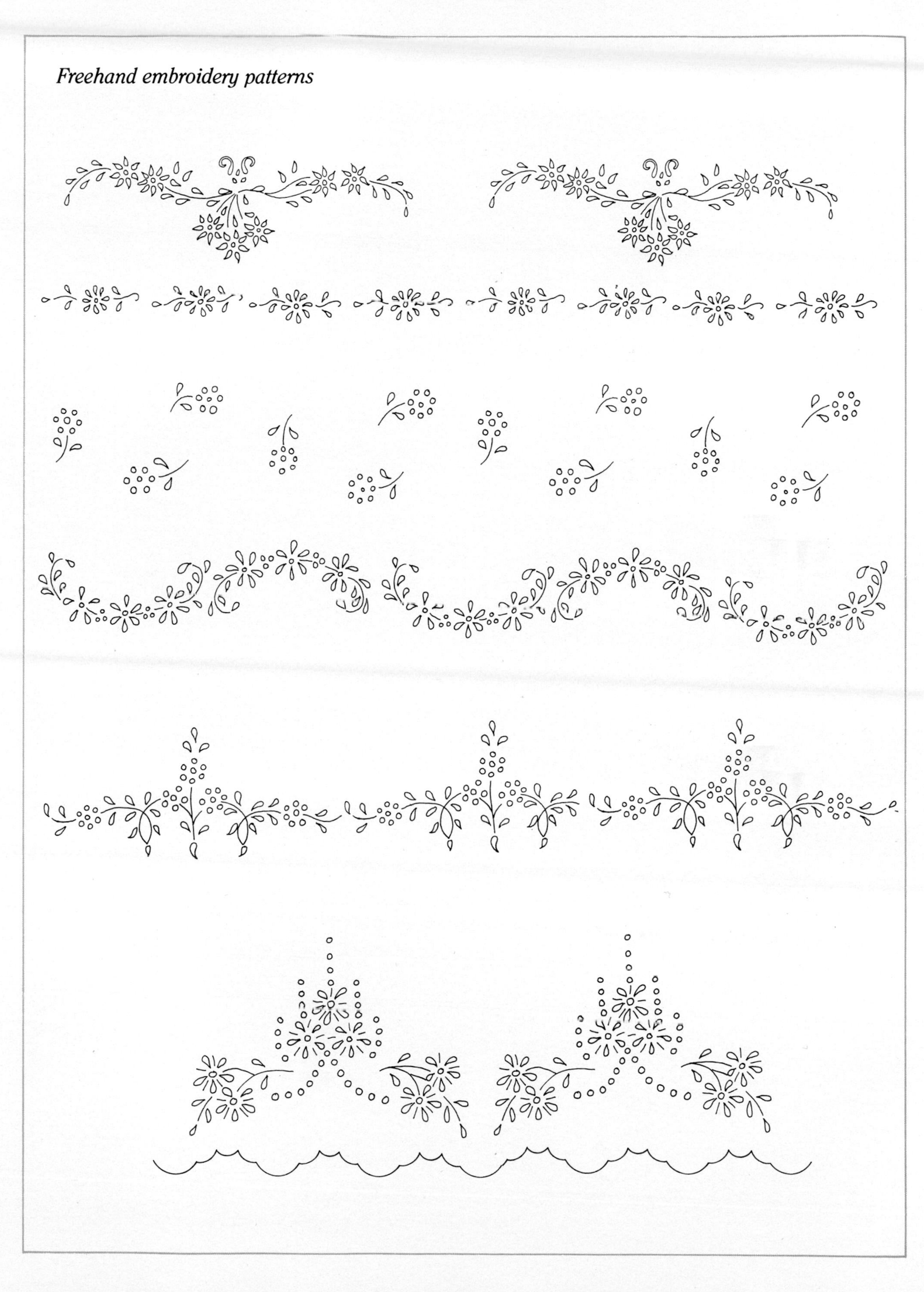
Freehand embroidery patterns

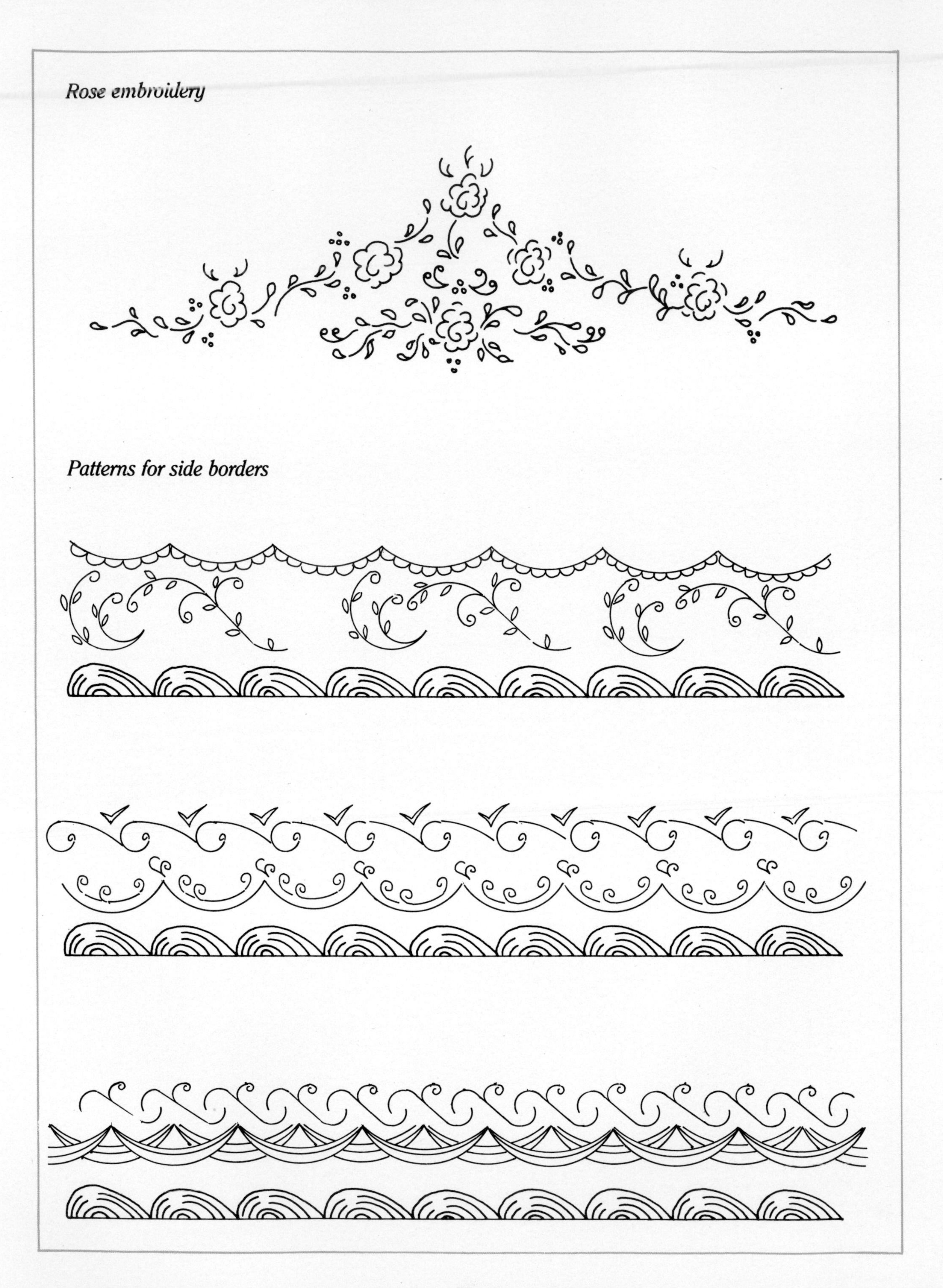
Rose embroidery
Patterns for side borders

Embroidered design

This lovely embroidery pattern has been used to advantage for this special cake for "Elizabeth", which features a beautiful Frangipani spray moulded in tropical fruit salad colours.

Side borders

Often these decorative side borders are effective when used in conjunction with the more masculine form of cake decorating, or depicted in the brighter colours around Christmas cakes. See page 20.

Elizabeth *is assured of a happy 21st with this lovely cake.*

Embroidery pattern used on Elizabeth *cake below.*

Embroidery patterns

Freehand piped lace

Lace made from royal icing should be piped through the finest tube that it is possible for the decorator to master. The finer the piping, the greater the risk of breakage when attaching the lace to the cake. For this reason, it is wise to make many more pieces than required.

1. Attach a piece of lined or graph paper to a small practice board. Cover it tautly with a piece of waxed paper, smoothing it down to ensure no bubbles appear. Secure it firmly with adhesive tape.
2. Now, with a soft peak consistency royal icing (see page 16) and No. 00 tube, pipe the selected lace design onto the waxed paper, using the lines from the paper underneath as a guide.
3. Allow the lace to dry thoroughly before removing the pieces with a fine steel spatula, knife or similar instrument.
4. The lace pieces are then attached to the cake or the top line of the extension border with a very small amount of royal icing.

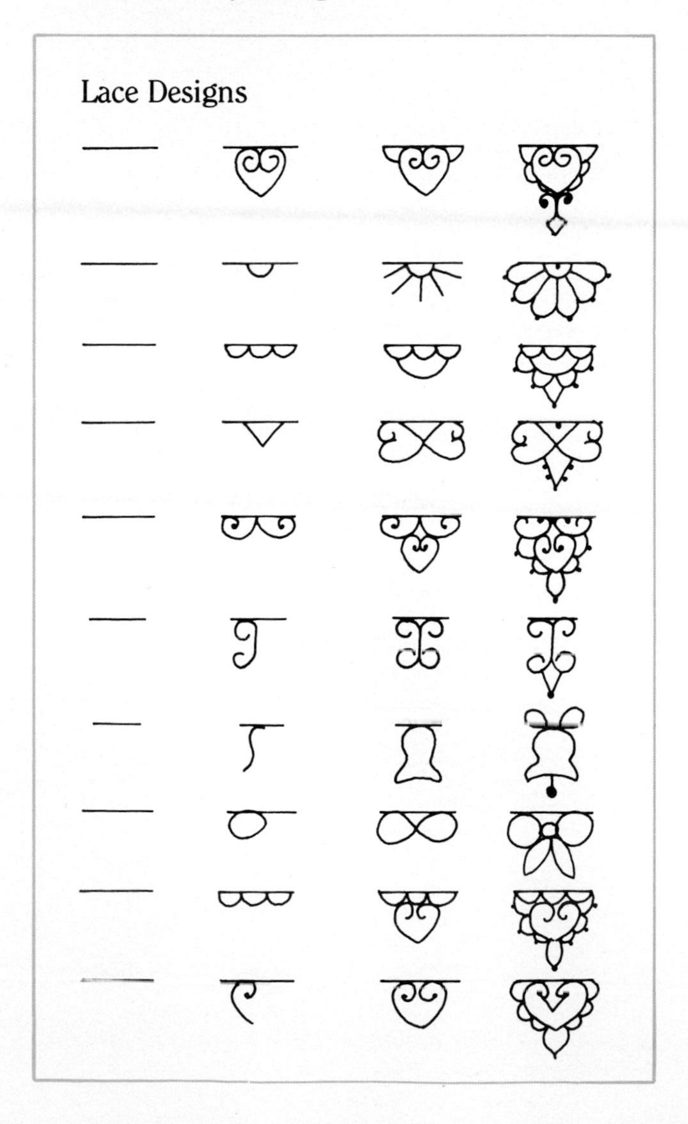

Figure piping lions head

1. Colour royal icing a buttercup yellow with a touch of brown. Place the icing into a piping bag with No. 3 tube and pipe a large ball for the head by keeping the hand pressure increased until the head is large enough.
2. Fill a paper cone with white royal icing and cut the point approximately the size of a No. 2 tube. Pipe 2 balls, side by side and in front of the head.

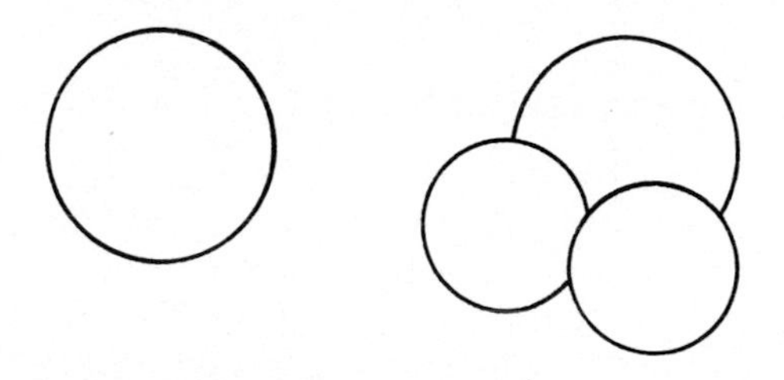

3. Pipe two small white balls at the top of the head for the inside of the ears.
4. With the No. 3 tube and buttercup/brown icing, pipe a long cylindrical nose, increasing the pressure towards the base, making it broader. Add a black tip to the nose.

5. Change again to the white icing and add two dots for the eyes, above the nose.
6. With the buttercup/brown icing, pipe around each white inside ear.
7. Paint the pupils of the eyes and the eyebrows in black. Paint a few black dots for the whiskers and pipe a red tongue.
8. Pipe on the mane — rough and tussled. Figure piping is a term which applies to pressure control of the piping medium within the bag, which when forced from the bag will hold a particular shape. It is usually done freehand without the aid of a pattern.

Clown Cake

To make these delightful clowns for a fun cake you will need sugar paste, royal icing and lengths of spaghetti.

Head

1. Take a piece of flesh-coloured fondant or modelling paste and shape it into a ball.
2. Break a length of spaghetti long enough for the body, plus the extra length required to push into the head.
3. Allow time to dry before painting in the funny face and piping on the tussled hair.

Body

1. Using a No. 8 tube and brightly coloured stiff royal icing, pipe the body around the length of the spaghetti stick from the neck until the rows piped are thick enough for the body size.
2. It is easier to accomplish this if the spaghetti is set into a piece of polystyrene over which has been placed a piece of waxed paper.

Arms/legs

1. Break the spaghetti into proportionate lengths for the upper and lower arms and likewise for the legs. Place the arm lengths into the wet icing of the body and pipe the full length of the arms with the No. 8 tube. Continue to pipe rows around the spaghetti as previously done for the body.
2. This same method is repeated for the legs.
3. Pipe the hands and the shoes from a small bag of icing.
4. Mould a funny hat for the head. Allow the clown to dry thoroughly before lifting it from the base.

Note: It is very important that children's novelties are all edible.

The Circus comes to Town *An exciting party time cake for the young. Clowns, figure piped animals, balloons and edible sawdust made from coloured coconut, make this cake enchanting.*

Floodwork (or run-in sugar)

The inspiration for this fascinating medium of cake decorating or sugar craft work invariably comes from special occasion cards, gift wrapping paper, children's story or painting books, badge motif designs, sporting magazines etc.

1. The royal icing is gradually thinned with drops of water (or egg white) until it reaches the consistency of clear honey.
2. The design to be copied may be traced from the original onto greaseproof paper and marked onto the covered cake, or the tracing may be secured to a firm supporting board then covered taughtly with waxed paper or freezer wrap.
3. Using a fine tube, outline the picture. Should the line break, join and continue, but touch the join with the tip of a fine paintbrush that has been moistened with water, to ensure there is no bump at the join.
4. Once the outline is dry, start filling in each section with the "flood royal" in the desired colours.
5. It is wise to study the picture closely in order that the fill-in sections are executed in their correct order. First fill the areas that are the furthest away from your vision and work your way forward, building the picture as you go.
6. The fill-in process may be done with a paper cone, or a bag fitted with a No. 1 tube. The alternative method is to apply the icing to each section with a small brush. In using either method the piped outline should be covered.

   The "brush flow" method may also be done without a piped outline. When using this method it is wise to allow drying time to adjoining colour sections.
7. For raised sections such as muscles, body contour, clothing or other specific features, extra icing is forced into the area by placing the tip of the bag under the surface of the floodwork and squeezing sufficiently to achieve the "rise" in the appropriate place. Once this "bulge" has been obtained, cease the pressure and remove the point of the bag from the work. (If necessary, smooth the surface lightly with a damp brush dipped in eggwhite).
8. A more pronounced 3-D look may be obtained by tracing extra arms, legs etc., flooding them separately, and allowing each to dry before attaching to the correct positions.
9. When the finished picture is completely dry, features such as eyes, eyelashes, shoes, belts and buttons may be painted on, as can highlights of light and shade.
10. Before removing the "flooded picture" from the board, consideration should be given to the background on the cake where the picture is to be applied.

    Specific details such as hills, trees and fences may need to be painted in with a paintbrush and food

Olde world charm of yesteryear is portrayed in this beautifully flooded cameo.

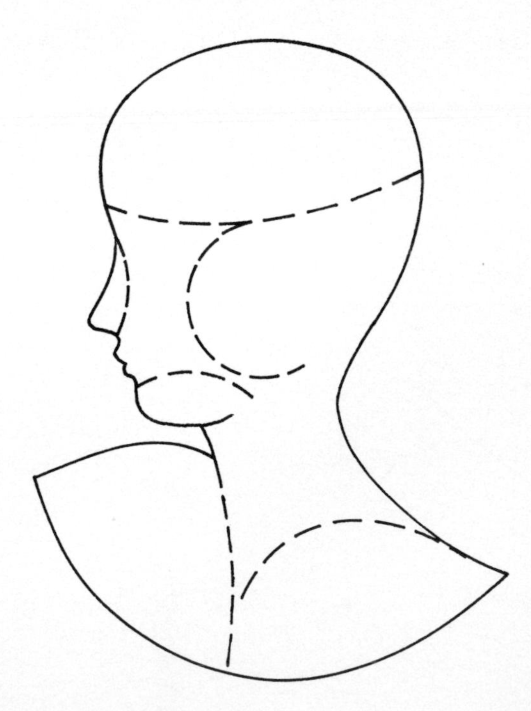

Contour lines indicate the more heavily flooded areas. See step 8.

colouring. Perhaps it may only be necessary to chalk dust some colour as a contrasting background to the picture, or a combination of both painting and chalk dusting may be applied.

11. Care should be exercised when removing the completely dried "flooded picture" from the work board. Once free, attach it with a little royal icing to the cake. *Do not* exert pressure on the floodwork otherwise it may break.

Note: Floodwork designs may also be applied directly to the cake's surface by pin pricking the outline of the tracing directly onto the cake.

Be My Valentine *The poodles in this delightful cake are a conbination of floodwork and small and large piped stars. A key code for the poodles apears on page 117.*

Flooding a base board

1. If the base board to be used under the cake is of a dark colour e.g. brown masonite, cover the entire surface with white contact adhesive paper.
2. Secure the cake to the board by placing a small quantity of royal icing, at normal consistency in the centre of the board before positioning the fondant-covered cake. Allow the cake to firm in this position before starting the flood work.
3. Transfer the board and cake to a turntable, then fill 2 large piping bags half to three-quarters full with flood consistency royal icing.
4. Cover the point of one bag with a damp cloth and cut the point of the other about the size of a No. 3 tube.
5. Flow the icing from the bag by maintaining an even pressure from the base of the cake to the edge of the board (or design of the collar).

6. Work alternately to the left and right of the floodwork, to avoid dry edges. Should air bubbles appear, break these immediately with a fine brush or pointed probe.
7. After the base board has been completely flooded, remove the board and cake from the turntable. Raise it a short height from the bench or table top and drop it squarely to the surface below. This bump should cause any hidden air bubbles to surface.
8. Clean the board edge of any icing runs and allow the floodwork to dry in a warm sunny position, or in a room with a dry heat such as a radiator. Remember to keep the cake a safe distance away from the heater.
9. When dry, the board edge may be neatened with a special narrow paper board trim, attached with royal icing as a facing to the edge of the board. Alternatively, it may be decorated by pipework from a tube such as a shell.
10. The cake is now ready to decorate.

Flooded board collar

1. Flooded board collars usually follow the same shape and design as that of the cake collar (see page 36).
2. Prepare and cover the board with the paper of your choice, or a fondant.
3. Having traced the collar design onto a piece of greaseproof paper, place this into position on the covered board and mark the design through. Remove the pattern.
4. Using No. 0 or 1 tube, pipe the design outline with royal icing onto the board.
5. Place a little royal icing into the centre of the board before lifting the covered cake into position. Allow to firm before starting to flood the collar area.
6. Follow the instructions given for flooding the board on page 27. Make sure to flood only from the cake base to the piped outline.
7. Additional pipework may be added as a decorative trim to the edge of the collar once it is completed.

Alternating method for floodwork

The process of alternating is to avoid the drying of edges in floodwork where large or complicated areas are involved. the example shown in the diagrams may be applied to numerous other shapes.

Alternating method for floodwork

Commence flooding at AA and proceed approximately 4 cm to BB, in a clockwise direction.

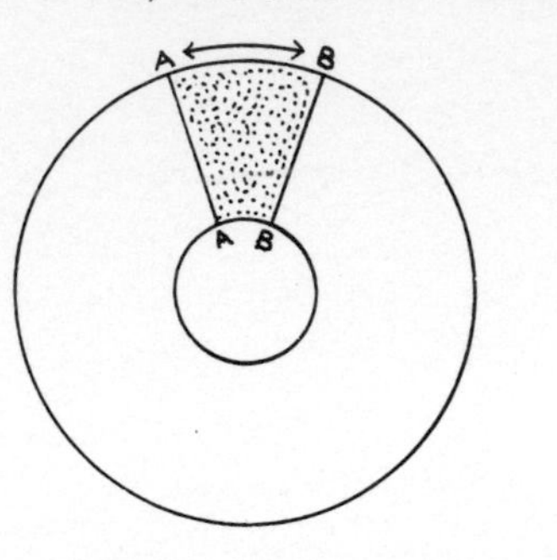

Return to AA and flood a similar short area to CC in an anticlockwise direction.

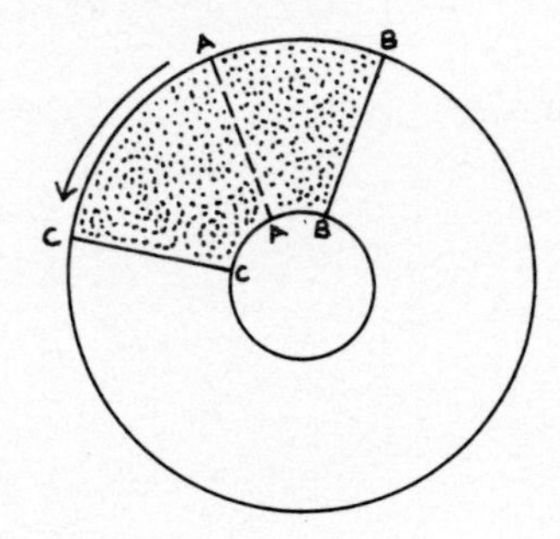

Flood clockwise from BB to DD.

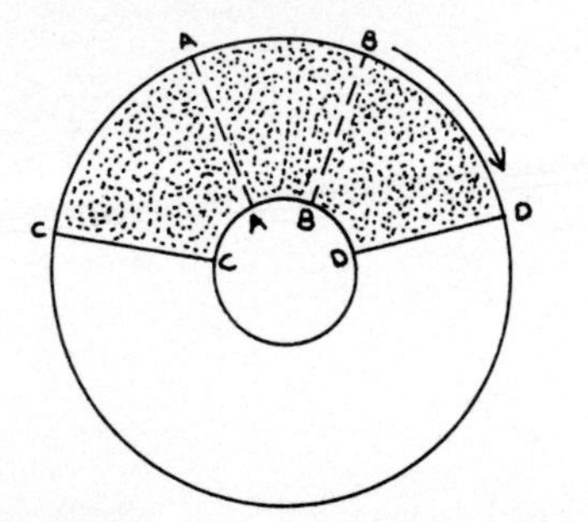

Flood anticlockwise from CC to EE and continue this reversing process until the required area is completely flooded.

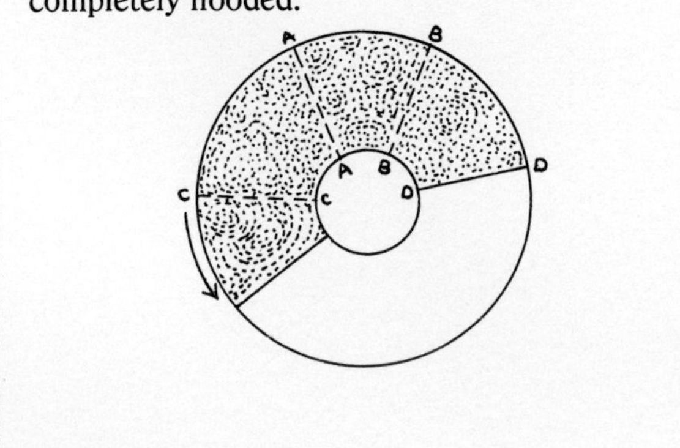

Christmas wreath

This bright festive wreath is easy to make. The size may vary from large to small according to the proportion of the cake, or it may be made as an individual plaque.

1. Cover a board with a piece of waxed paper or freezer wrap. Attach it firmly with adhesive tape.
2. Divide royal icing at "soft peak" consistency into separate portions and colour each with a bright fruit colour such as orange, red, yellow and violet. Pipe apples, oranges, apricots, pears, bananas, cherries, grapes etc. onto the waxed paper. Touch each piece of piped fruit with a paintbrush dipped in egg white to give a smooth surface. When dry, paint in any details such as shading, stems and the brown markings on the bananas. Allow to dry.

   Note: Fruits may also be piped in white royal icing and painted later.
3. Cover another board as above. Freehand pipe green royal icing from a No. 0 or 1 tube to form many pine needles and ferns and allow to dry.
4. Using green modelling paste, roll, cut and vein pairs of holly leaves in various sizes. Cutters may be used for this purpose or the shape of the leaves traced from a card and cut by pattern. Roll tiny balls of red paste for the berries. Allow three berries for each pair of holly leaves. Allow all pieces to dry. Brush fruit, leaves and berries with edible glaze, see page 112.

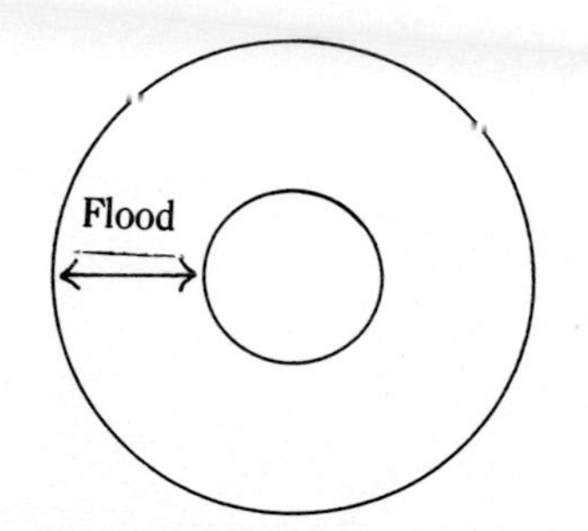

To assemble

Cut out modelling paste into the required size circle if the wreath is to be used as a plaque, or alternatively mark the area of the circle onto the cake.

Flood the area between the outer and inner circle with green royal icing and place the fruit, pine needles, ferns, holly leaves and berries into position, elevating some and leaving some flat. Be sure to fill in the gaps.

Tie a ribbon bow at the top of the circle and attach a cluster of Christmas bush and Christmas bells (see pages 69 and 70). This may be omitted and replaced with a sugar paste card with greetings inscribed.

SPECIAL TECHNIQUES

Bas-relief or sculptured fondant

Bas-relief or sculptured fondant is a technique used to produce two-dimensional decorations. Figures are given a life-like appearance by having their facial and body contours "built up". Clothes may be applied as fitted or flared, thus presenting a most natural effect.

Bas-relief involves painting, especially where faces are viewed full on, rather than in profile; eye expression is very important. Background shading is required for contrast and greater visual appeal.

While some bas-relief designs can be time consuming, the task is a real pleasure.

Sugar and spice (girl and boy)

These two cuties have been developed from the bas-relief or sculptured fondant technique.

Sugar and spice, presented here, is the work of the very talented South African cake decorator, Jeanette Van Niekerk. Pattern pieces for both girl and boy will be found on page 119. Follow the working sequence set out for optimum results.

Sugar (girl)

Colour small portions of the fondant with the desired shades for the body and the clothes.

Trace the pattern and transfer it to the cake or plaque. Alternatively, place the pattern under a sheet of glass or perspex and outline it in royal icing with No. 0 or 1 tube. Allow this outline to dry, then reverse the glass and press down onto the soft surface of the covered cake or plaque, thus indenting the pattern.

Note: By this method the picture will face the opposite direction.

Build head, face and body contours with small pieces of fondant. Then, by dampening each piece, attach them to the various areas of the pattern. Flatten all outer edges to avoid a ridge showing.

Order of work

1. *Shoes:* Use two equal-sized balls of fondant approximately 8 mm in circumference. Shape these and attach in correct position.
2. *Pantaloons:* Roll out a long strip of fondant. With a cocktail stick frill the lower edge that extends over the shoes. Dampen each leg and attach.
3. *Petticoat:* Roll the fondant thinly and cut the pattern. Frill the hemline. Roll a narrow piece of fondant and cut a strip approximately 3 mm wide. Frill along one edge and attach just above frill of petticoat.
4. *Skirt:* Roll and cut pattern. Dampen along the side seams and across the waistline. Attach it to the petticoat. Allow the skirt to fall in natural folds.
5. *Bodice:* Roll and cut the pattern and attach it to the body.
6. *Apron:* Roll and cut according to pattern. Make a few pleats or folds at the waistline and place it in position, then cut the top of the apron and attach.
7. *Arms:* Roll out a long sausage shape and cut it to size. Dampen both arms and attach them to the body.
8. *Apron frill:* Frill the outer edges that protrude over each arm. Pleat slightly and attach it to the apron.
9. *Hands:* Make two even-sized pieces of fondant into a carrot or teardrop shape. Flatten the front and cut the fingers, bending them to give a natural look. Attach hands into the sleeves by dampening around wrists.

Bride and Groom mouse wedding cake *This delightful cake features the "Gill Heinrich ribbon appliqué border" a sheer beauty by its originator Gill, the lovely sprays adorning the cake are a group effort by members of the Cake Decorators Association of South Australia. Instructions for moulded mice are on Page 52 and Appliqué ribbon on page 44.*

These examples of bas relief would be most suitable for either a little boy or girl's birthday cake or the angels for a Christmas cake. See pages 118 - 121 for templates.

Springtime is Funtime

Bluebird on My Finger

Sugar and Spice

Someone's Halo is Slipping

10. *Ice-cream cone:* This is shaped and placed into Sugar's right hand. Pipe royal icing into cone for ice-cream.

11. *Face:* Cut out according to the pattern and place into position after dampening. For the nose, attach a tiny ball of fondant into position.

    Paint the outline of the eyes and colour the ball of eye, leaving a white highlight. Deepen the pupil.

    Attach a small frill around neck to hide the join of the head to the body.

12. *Hair:* Use a No. 1 tube and royal icing.

Finishing touches: Flowers or dots may be piped or painted onto the dress and apron. Fondant bow may be attached to the hair.

Spice (boy)

Follow as directed for the girl in this working order.

1. Shoes
2. Shirt
3. Pants
4. Sleeves
5. Arms
6. Straps for pants
7. Face
8. Cap
9. Hair
10. Finishing touches

It's a Boy *However, this christening cake featuring the Garrett frill is suitable for a boy or girl.*

Garrett frill and embroidery.

Garrett frill

This versatile technique was devised by South African decorator, Elaine Garrett, after whom it was named.

It is possible to purchase special cutters for this work; however the same results may be achieved by using a large and small round pastry cutter. The small inside cutter should be plain-edged, the large cutter should be scalloped. Sizes will vary according to the design.

1. Roll out the fondant and cut out a circle using the cutter.
2. For ease in handling and applying the frill, it is better to cut the circle in half (see diagram 2, page 35). Cover one half to prevent it drying while working on the other.
3. Using a cocktail stick, press it firmly into the scalloped edge of the fondant. Work along the edge pressing the stick into the fondant, side by side with each previously made groove, until the scalloped edge of the half circle is fully indented. Place the cocktail stick under the "frilled" edge and raise this edge at intervals to form a soft fluting.
4. To apply to the cake, dampen the back of the top edge with water, turn about 5 mm of the right hand side end of the scallop under towards the cake and place the frill into position.
5. Repeat this method with the remaining half scallop and subsequent scallops, taking care to camouflage each join by folding the left hand edge of the scallop neatly over the turned-under right edge of the previous scallop. Allow it to fall softly into a "frill" at the point of the join.

The flounce

This is a softer version of the *Garrett frill* and is produced by rolling a suitable tool such as a knitting needle along the edge in a forward and backward movement until the edge flutes softly.

Lift the edge slightly by placing the tool under it to raise the fluted edge. Attach the flounce to the cake as previously explained for the "frill".

The cone-shaped frill

1. Cut out a fondant strip with a scalloped base.
2. Make a mark at the height desired for the apex from the centre of each scallop (see diagram 5, page 35).
3. Using a cocktail stick, press a groove into the fondant from the apex to the centre of the scallop. Then, working on either side of that centre line, mark a series of indentations with the cocktail stick, progressively reducing the length of each line, so that the top of the cone forms a straight edge from the apex to the point of the scallop.
4. Each cone should be completed separately and immediately lifted beneath it with the cocktail stick to allow it to flute.

Cocoa painting

Cocoa painting may be applied directly onto the cake's surface or onto a plaque.

It is necessary to have a selection of pure hair paint-brushes, ranging in size from No. 000 to 3. Use the finest brush for outline work and the thicker ones for filling in. The monochromatic shades look spectacular if well

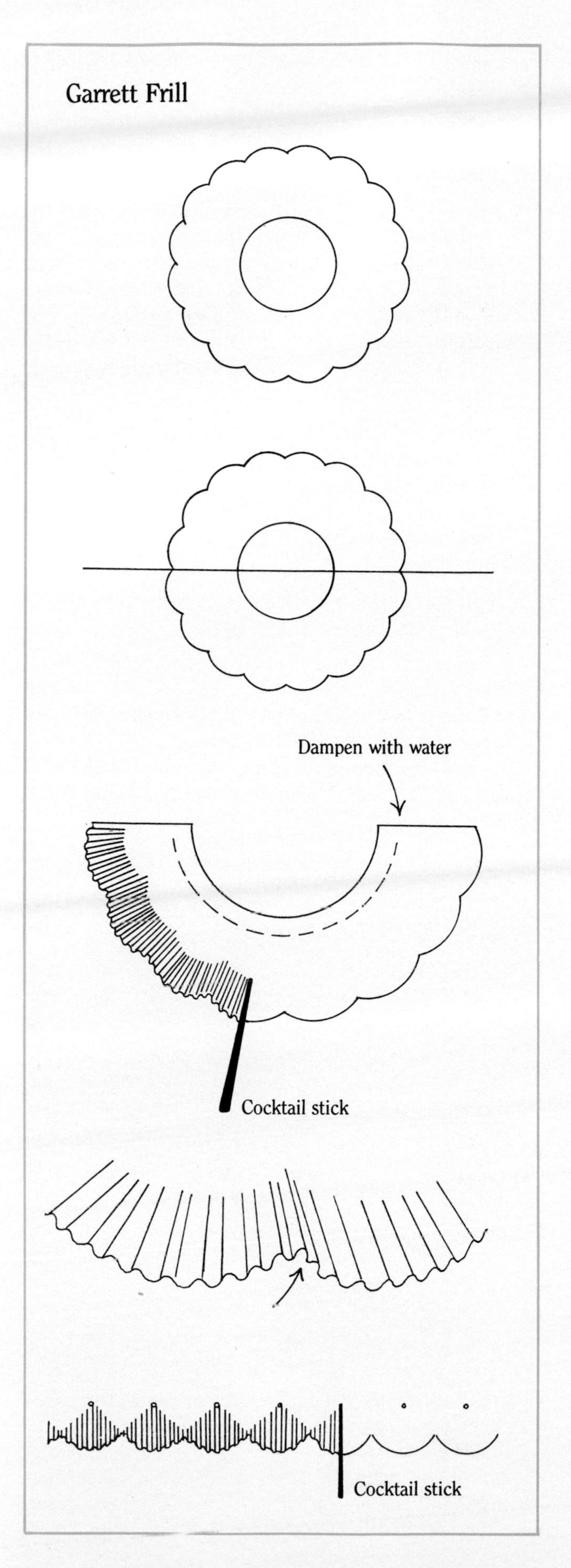

applied, showing light and dark, and highlighting the areas according to the light source.

1. Trace the design.
2. Place hot water into the lower pan of a container similar to an egg poacher.
3. Place ½ teaspoon cocoa butter (Oil Theobroma) over the hot water, in one of the egg trays.
4. Place approximately 1 teaspoon dry cocoa into one of the unused egg trays.
5. Dip the fine brush into the melted cocoa butter, then into the dry cocoa powder and blend it well on the side of the pan until a dark or light shade has been achieved.
6. Paint in the outline work with a fine brush. Then fill in the other details with the heavier brushes, showing light and dark shadings and emphasising highlights.
7. Should the cocoa butter begin to thicken, reheat or renew the hot water. Do not allow the brush to become heavy with thickened butter. Oil Theobroma (cocoa butter) is very expensive and should not be wasted (it is obtainable from chemists). While practising this technique, white vegetable shortening may be used until the decorator gains confidence and experience.

   Note: If mistakes occur, remove them with a piece of dry cotton wool or a dry cotton bud.
8. The decorator may find it easier to build up the colours and highlights by first filling in completely with the palest shade, then painting in the areas of medium colour before brushing in the darkest toning where required.
9. Should the highlights of the eyes be lost in the process of painting, these may be regained by carefully lifting part of the surface coating of the eye with a sharp scalpel where the highlights are required.
10. To produce a fur effect, lightly scratch the surface with the point of a cocktail stick or similar object.

Plaque showing cocoa painted motif on squirrel and bird.

Collar work

Beautiful collars of royal icing used in the decoration of both cake and base board, are mainly associated with English decorators. Due to their outstanding skill and expertise, this method of sugar work has become popular in many countries. (See pages 122 and 123 for collar patterns.)

1. The collar should be planned and drawn on a piece of firm greaseproof paper. The width of the collar should overlap the cake by an equal margin.
2. It is wise to draw the size of the tin in which the cake has been baked, onto the greaseproof paper. This will be referred to as the "cake line". Mark a line approximately 2 cm to the inside and 2 cm to the outside of the "cake line" (see page 122).
3. Should a repetitive pattern be designed for the outer edge such as scallops or a geometric design, fold the greaseproof paper pattern into the number of equal portions required, mark the shape of the edge onto the pattern and cut cleanly with scissors while the pattern is still folded. The inside edge may have the same pattern as the outside, or it may be left as a plain line.
4. Collars are often quite fancy in design. Cut-outs, known as "windows", may be included. These are later piped with lattice, embroidery or scroll work or made even more detailed by introducing names or greetings.
5. Once the collar pattern has been completed, cut it out and place it onto the cake, in order to see the effect and balance.
6. On a new sheet of greaseproof paper re-trace the collar pattern. Do not cut this sheet of paper, but allow a good margin beyond the drawing in order that this may be firmly attached with adhesive tape to a larger board, sheet of glass or perspex. The pattern, once attached, should remain perfectly flat with no bubbles, otherwise the collar will be uneven when completed.
7. Once the pattern is secure, give a light brushing all over with white vegetable oil. Over this apply a sheet of waxed paper, also smeared lightly with the vegetable oil. Care must be taken to ensure the waxed paper is also perfectly flat, smooth and without creases.
8. Using a No. 0 or 1 tube and royal icing, pipe over all lines pertaining to the design.

This tailored cake features both top and board collars and is complimented by the beautiful spray of Chrysanthemums and wild violets. Templates for these collars and for a Royal collar are on pages 122 and 123.

The ever popular petal shaped cake has a simple elegance. This one combines the beautiful Bougainvillea, scalloped filigree lace and flooded royal board collar to perfection.

9. The breakdown of royal icing for floodwork, often referred to as run-in sugar or flow work, must be done with care, by adding the thinning medium slowly (my preference is water). Add water gradually, almost drop by drop; do not beat but mix slowly and well after each addition of water until the mixture has a sluggish, syrup consistency.
10. If the mixture is too wet it will delay the drying and may cause the paper to buckle underneath. Air bubbles will increase if the mixture is too thin. Always allow the icing to stand for a while before use. This will allow any air bubbles to rise to the surface. A gentle stir will eliminate most of these.
11. Before starting the flood work (run-in), be sure to break down ample royal icing to complete the collar without having to pause to re-mix. It is better to have mixture over, than not enough.
12. A piping bag, paper cone, spoon or paintbrush may be used to flow the icing between the outline work of the pattern, working between the inside and outside edges in a quick and systematic manner, changing ends after approximately every 4 cm of work, so that neither end has time to dry until the collar is completed. The decorator will find a fine paintbrush beneficial to push the icing into small corners and to assist in breaking air bubbles that may appear on the surface.
13. Allow to dry quickly in a sunny position or in front of a radiator to ensure a gloss. When removing the collar from the paper, hold it in front of a room heater until the vegetable shortening softens, then slide off.
14. Collar work, when used around the base board of the cake should follow the same shape as the one above.

Note: If using a dark base board such as masonite, cover the area to be flooded for the collar with white contact adhesive. This will prevent a stain seeping through the sugar after the run-in work has been completed.

Attaching the collar to the top cake

Using No. 2 tube, drop lines, row upon row over the "cake line" on the cake to form a wall of the desired height. Allow to firm. Pipe another row and attach the collar to the wet icing.

Crimping

Crimpers are also known as clippers and are available in many sizes and designs. Three of the most popular are the single scallop, double scallop and "Vee". ◡ ◡◡ ∨

Many so-called crimpers are designed to imprint a pattern onto the fondant, without pinching and raising a ridge. An example of these are the heart and petal shaped crimpers ♡ ◯ whose prongs do not meet completely. True crimpers meet together, by one prong fitting into the line of the other for the full width of the implement.

When correctly inserted into the cake at right angles, they will pinch a neat ridged pattern onto the surface at regular intervals. This requires practice, but once mastered, the technique provides the beginner as well as the advanced decorator with a quick method of repetitive design which, when applied to the top, sides and borders of special occasion cakes, accompanied by additional pipework, produces a most professional finish.

Use of crimpers

1. Crimping must be carried out immediately, on freshly applied fondant.
2. To prevent the crimpers from sticking, dip the serrated edges in cornflour.
3. Shake, to remove any excess cornflour, then hold the crimper firmly between the thumb, index finger and middle finger at right angles to the cake, with a space between the crimper prongs of approximately 3 mm.
4. Insert the ends into the fondant a little deeper than the serrated edges. Squeeze slightly to pinch the ridge, yet not completely together; otherwise the piece will pull away with the crimpers, leaving a gap.

Season's Greetings *Bright and cheery this Christmas cake features crimper work and ribbon insertion. Poinsettia and Cotoneaster feature in the showy spray.*

5. In order to remove the crimper cleanly and without damage to the cakes surface, ease the pressure slightly and lift away from the crimped ridge.

   Note: If the pressure is released too soon while the crimpers are still in the fondant, it will result in large stretch teeth marks across the work, which will spoil the appearance and prove impossible to hide.

6. Crimper work is incomplete unless the design is then over-piped or decorated with royal icing. This may take the form of plain piped lines, scallops, dots, roping, snails trail and embroidery from the finer tubes.

Note: Many decorators may find it easier to gain even "ridges" by wrapping an elastic band around the crimpers, approximately 3 cm from the serrated edge. Apply the band tightly enough to provide a space 3mm between the prongs.

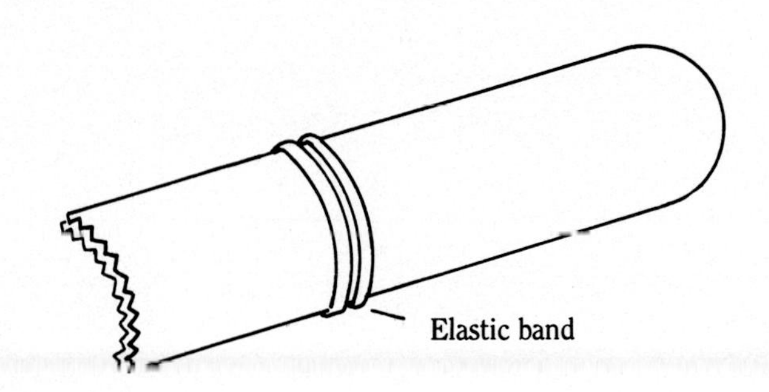

Crimpers

Extension work

Extension work is a piping skill which requires many hours of practice by the decorator. This beautiful work is more commonly used for border designs and bridgework support for floating collars and should be executed with the greatest of care to achieve perfection.

To carry out this technique, the decorator must first master the handling of tubes as fine as the No. 000, 00 or the special No. 0000, which has been fitted with a hypodermic needle to produce the finest of piping.

1. Measure a paper template accurately around the circumference of the covered cake. Then remove it and fold it evenly into the required number of panels or sections necessary for the design.
2. Mark the design onto the template, cut the base edge along the scalloped line, and pin the template back into position around the cake.
3. Prick any guidelines of the design or pattern onto the cake before removing the template.

Note: Always keep the base scallops (or base design) as close to the board as possible without touching. The more shallow the scallop the neater the base line will be.

4. Neaten the cake base edge with a fine teardrop or snails trail piped with No. 00 or 0 tube. (Shell tubes are not recommended, no matter how small, as they appear heavy beneath such dainty work).
5. With a No. 2 tube, begin to pipe the first row of the extension base scallop. (See page 40)
6. Allow time for each row to dry (or firm) before piping the next one directly over the previous row. Gaps should not appear between the rows. This will depend greatly on how perfect the cake cover was to start, and whether it was of an even thickness, showing no undulations. It will also depend upon the experience and skill of the decorator.
7. Continue piping until 5 or 6 rows have been completed. Allow the extension work to dry before beginning the bridgework (see page 40).

Bridgework (or drop thread work)

This is a bridging from the side of the cake to the base extension; or the piped lines may form a bridge of support from a floating collar to the cake (see page 40).

Use the finest tube possible such as No. 000 or 00, or, depending upon the decorator's expertise, No. 0000.

1. Drop a vertical line from the top edge of the border to the base extension line, keeping an even pressure on the piping bag to avoid the icing thread from breaking. Continue to carry the line just under the extension base.
2. The next vertical line should be piped so close to the previous one as to make it impossible to pipe another into the space between the bridgework (or thread).

Extension and Bridgework

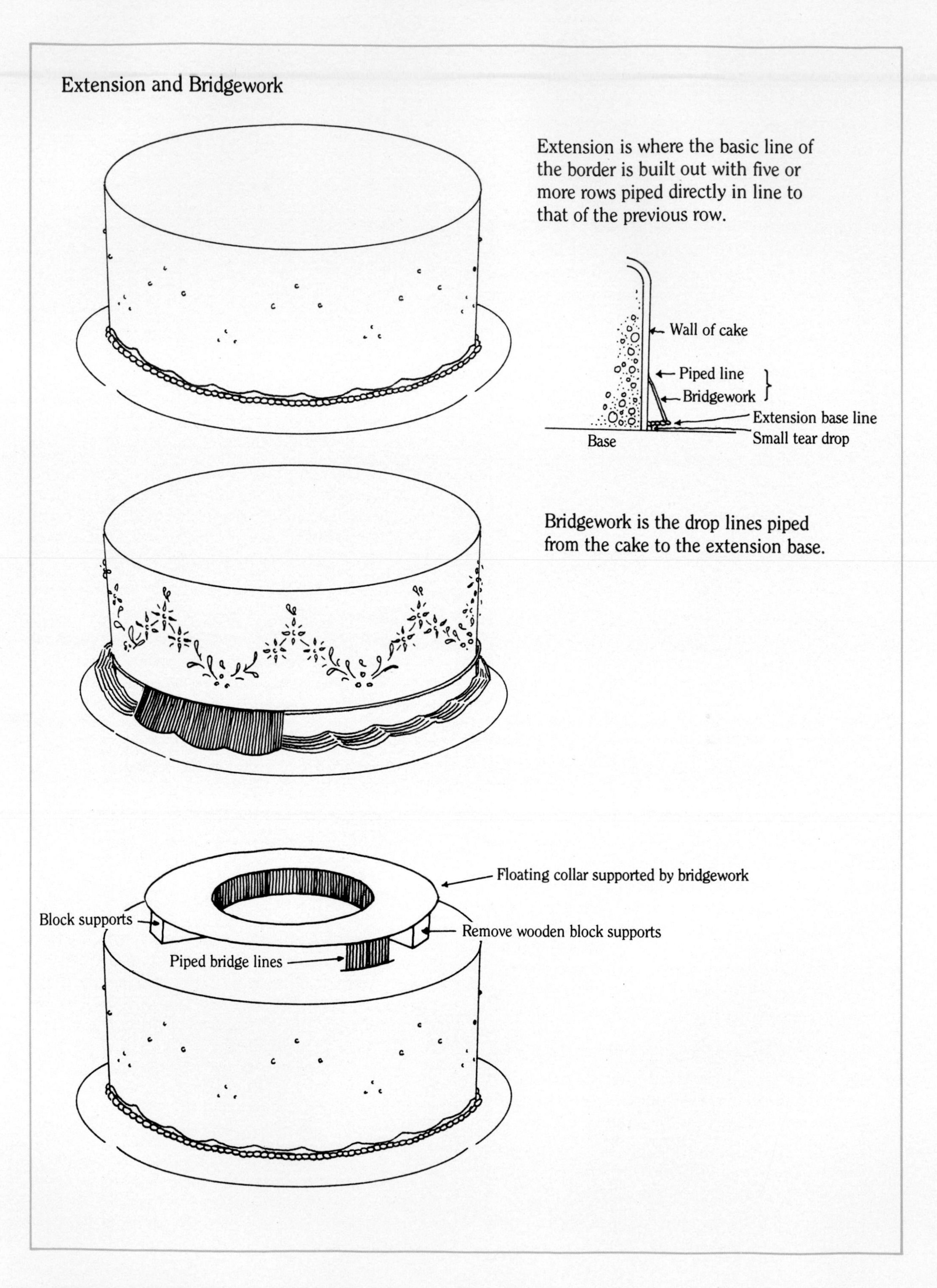

This technique is for the skilled decorator. Piping perfection is essential to gain this difficult border.

3. In the continuous execution of this pipework, if the drop lines touch or break, they must be removed. A fine paintbrush is useful in this respect and for keeping tidy any edges that may appear below the extension base from the bridgework.
4. The top of the border may be neatened with free standing lace which has been previously piped on waxed paper and allowed to dry before being removed and attached to the cake with a little royal icing.

Alternatively, a lace trim of scallops may also be piped directly along the top edge of the bridgework to neaten and finish that line. Small piped scallops or a plain piped line may also neaten the base line of the extension.

It has become commercially acceptable to over-flood the built out rows of the extension prior to doing the bridgework. This method does add extra strength to the work. It also covers a multitude of mistakes.

From a judging point of view, for the decorator anticipating show or exhibition work, it must be understood that the judge/s, in assessing the exhibit, like to see the piping ability of the exhibitor. In a closely contested section, the judge should award a higher point to the decorator who shows her ability with the pipework in preference to the work covered with royal icing, probably used to camouflage poor work.

Pleated extension

1. Measure the circumference of the cake accurately. Then divide the length evenly to make each "pleat" the exact same size. Mark onto the cake.
2. With royal icing and the No. 2 tube begin by piping a small teardrop to the left of each "pleat" mark.
3. Start the next row a little to the right of the first teardrop, and pipe exactly along the edge of the first row, extending longer to the left along the cake.
4. Repeat, making each row extend longer to the left until the marked space is complete with a slanted shelf of extension, approximately six deep.
5. Be sure each outside line is smooth and straight. Allow to dry.
6. Begin the drop thread work (bridgework) by piping a straight line into the crevice. Pipe about 9 lines from each crevice and when all have been done around the cake continue to follow on along each "pleat" until the point of the next pleat is reached.

   It is only possible to pipe one or two lines around this point.
7. One piece of lace, the width of the bridgework, is attached to the top of each "pleat".
8. Finish the bottom of the extension shelf by piping a small picot or tiny scallops.

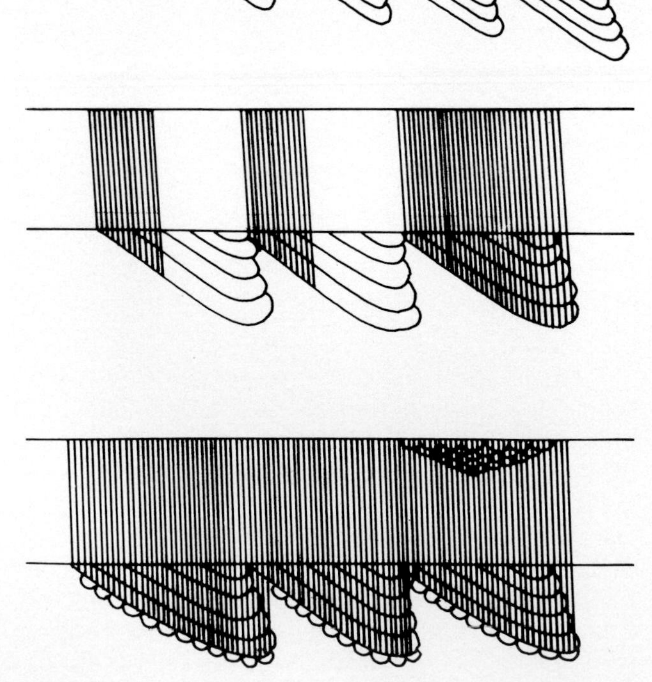

Ribbon insertion

Ribbon insertion complements crimper work.

1. Select the width and colour of the ribbon. The colour may be in definite contrast with that of the cake, or toned a shade deeper than the cake covering. Satin ribbon has the most appeal when used for this work.
2. Start by crimping the pattern onto the cake covering.
3. Cut the ribbon into short lengths approximately 1 cm.
4. Cut slits in the fondant with a sharp scalpel above the line of crimping, to correspond with the width of the ribbon.
5. Using a pair of pointed tweezers, pick up one ribbon piece at a time, fold it in half and insert the two open ends of the ribbon jointly into the slit.
6. Embed it into the fondant until it is exactly level with the surface of the covering, no more, no less. This will ensure an appealing and neat finish.

Note: The ribbon lengths may vary according to the style of the insertion, e.g. where a double slit is cut, this will lengthen the ribbon accordingly.

With this method, only one end of the ribbon is inserted into the first slit with the aid of the tweezers, before inserting the other end into the second slit.

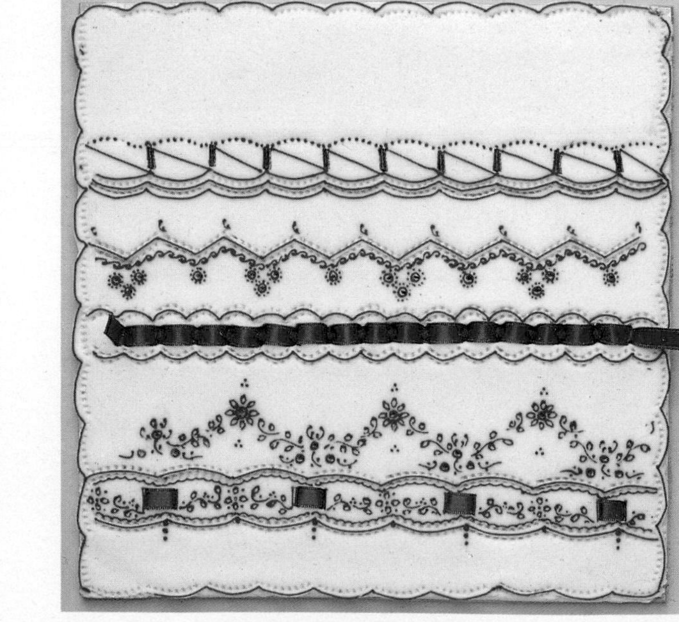

Examples of crimper work and ribbon insertion.

Pleated extension of this three tier wedding cake shows the skill of its decorator, Mavis Mepham.

The continuous ribbon method

1. Measure the length of the ribbon around the cake and allow half as much length again.
2. Crimp the design, allowing sufficient space between the two rows to take the width of the ribbon. Crimp the base scallop line first, then reverse the crimper to form a border of the desired width.
3. With a pair of pointed tweezers, or a semi-pointed tool, poke the end of the ribbon into the fondant at the scallop's closest point.

   Allow some slack to the ribbon before inserting it into the next section to avoid pulling the ribbon out of the fondant from the previous "poked" hole.
4. Repeat this process continuously around the cake.
5. To secure the ribbon into position, pipe a reasonably sized dot into each "poke" hole.

Eyelet embroidery

Eyelet embroidery when used with crimper work is most effective. Designs vary from the simple to the very decorative. Whereas crimping should be done immediately the fondant has been applied, eyelet holes may be marked an hour or so later, after the fondant has firmed a little.

1. A clear plan of the design should be worked out first, before poking holes at random into the cake. Mistakes cannot be hidden.
2. Use the point of a knitting needle or similar tool. Push into the fondant sufficiently to give a distinct hole. There is no need to go too deep. Each hole requires piping around the edge with No. 00 or 0 tube. This provides a good centre from which to form a piped flower or embroidery of choice (see pages 19, 33 and 42).

Ribbon appliqué

This technique, combining ribbon with extension work, was originated by Gill Heinrich, one of South Australia's talented cake decorators. It has been my privilege and pleasure to name this work "the Heinrich method of ribbon applique" after its originator.

1. Measure and carefully mark the design on graph paper. Accuracy is essential. Then trace the pattern onto greaseproof paper and mark it on the cake. Base scallops should be close to the board.
2. Neaten the base of the cake with a small piped "teardrop" or "snails trail".
3. Using the No. 1 or 2 tube, pipe the base scallop (extension). Allow it time to firm or dry before piping the next line directly over it. Repeat this method until four rows have been completed.
4. Then pipe the row of scallops above this line, until three rows have been completed. Allow drying time as before.
5. Cut each ribbon appliqué pattern individually, to maintain the perfect fit required when attaching to the design.

Detail of the wedding cake on page 31.

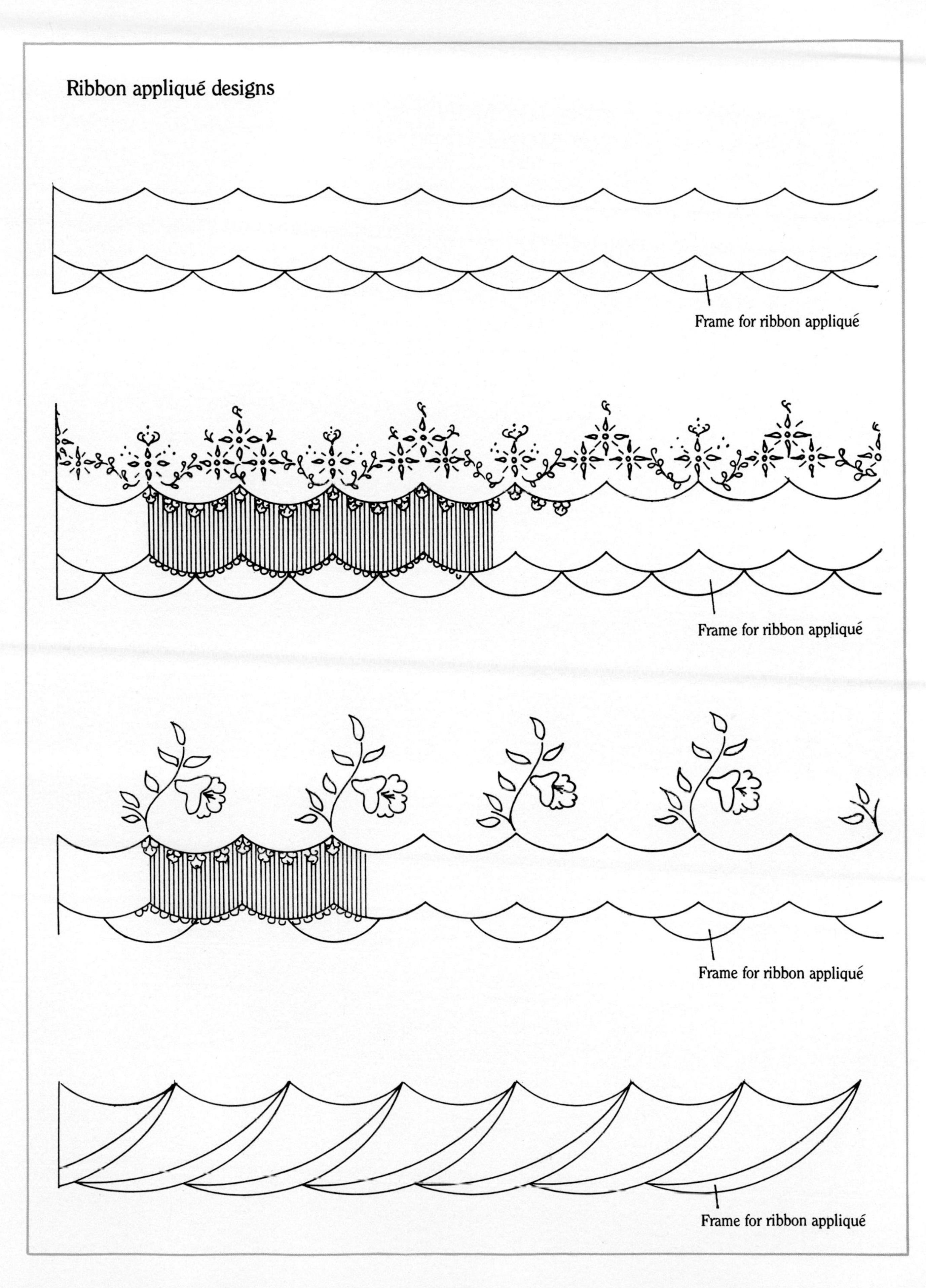
Ribbon appliqué designs
Frame for ribbon appliqué
Frame for ribbon appliqué
Frame for ribbon appliqué
Frame for ribbon appliqué

6. Pipe one row of royal icing around the section to which the ribbon is to be applied. Lift the satin piece with the aid of tweezers and place it into position over the wet royal icing.
7. Press it into position with a dry paintbrush. Continue to do each section for the ribbon separately. Do not pipe more than one section at a time, otherwise the icing will dry before the ribbon can be attached.
8. With a No. 0 tube, pipe a continuous row of scallops above the ribbon and directly over the previously piped rows of three.
9. Using a No. 000 or 00 tube, begin to pipe the bridgework (or drop thread lines) from the cake cover to the extension border above the ribbon.

   Take care when piping not to drop icing onto the ribbon as this will spoil the effect. Have a damp brush ready to remove these marks immediately, should it be necessary.
10. When the bridgework is completed, pipe over the top and bottom line of scallops to neaten off using No. 000 or 00 tube.
11. Finish the top edge of the bridgework by attaching piped pieces of lace (see page 45).

Mothers day cake

Ribbon appliqué between two borders of bridgework provides a most interesting and attractive base.

1. Follow the instructions as described on page 39. However, when marking the pattern onto the cake, leave at least 1.5 cm from the lower scallop line to the base board.
2. When the step-by-step work has been completed up to and including step 9, start to pipe the lower bridgework from the lower edge of the appliqued border to the base board of the cake, to form a border about 2 cm out from the cake.

This special Mothers Day cake features a dainty floral arrangement of climbing geraniums and wild violets. Appliqué ribbon between two borders of bridgework provides an attractive base.

The Endeavour *combining flood work and the Heinrich technique of ribbon appliqué in the sails.*

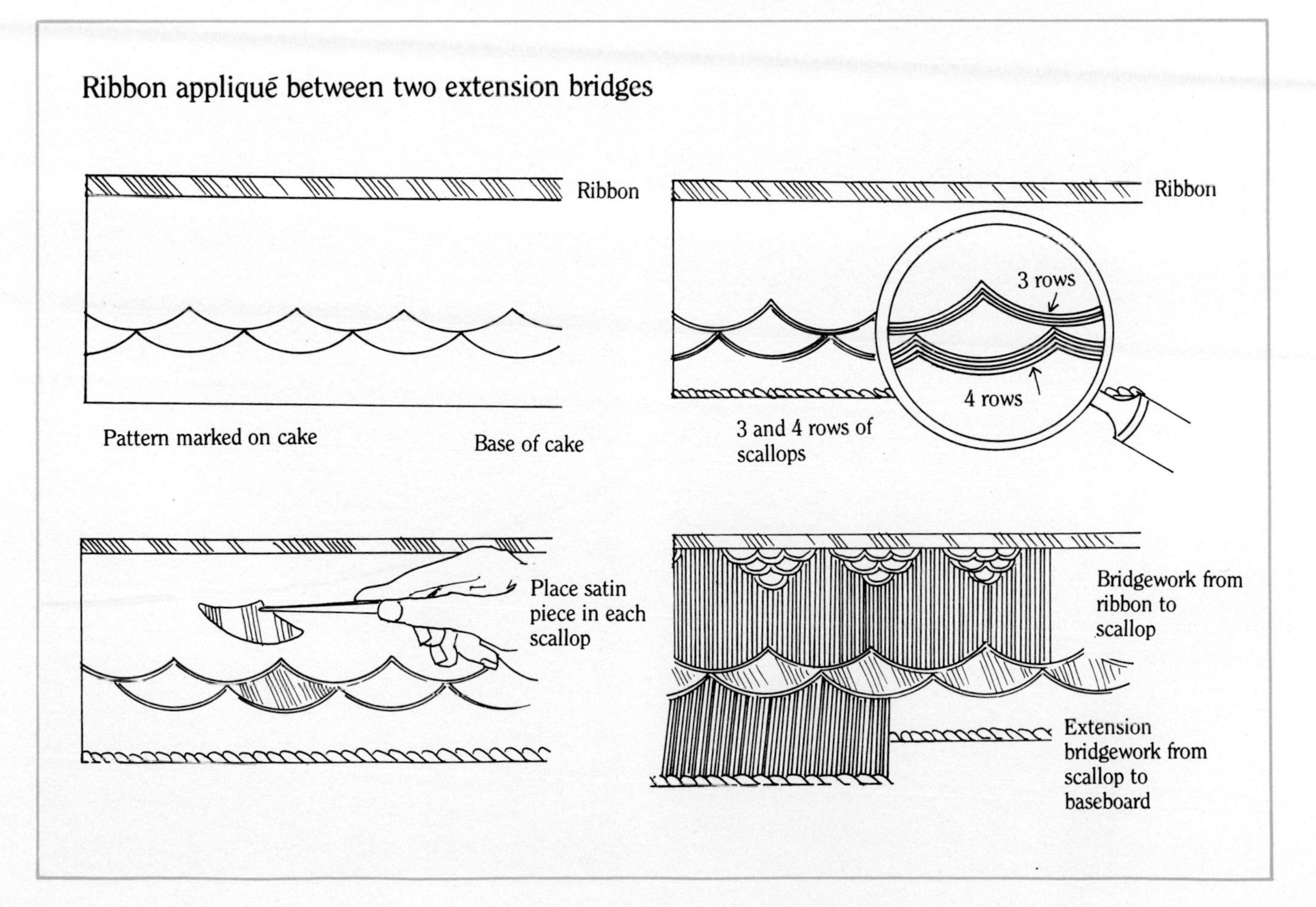

Hollow linc work

This is an old technique enjoying new popularity. Each line is built out on a slant from the outside edges of the pattern, until they meet in the centre to form a hollow scroll or trumpet.

This interesting technique may be used to decorate the sides or top of special occasion cakes and may be piped directly onto the surface or over a sheet of waxed paper and lifted off and placed into position.

1. Trace out the pattern and transfer it to the cake. Lightly mark the outline and remove the pattern.
2. With a No. 00 or 0 tube, pipe from the outside lines **A** and **B** and allow to dry (or firm) before piping the next line over the first, placing it a little to the side and slanting it towards the centre. Each line thus piped with be slightly shorter than the one before.
3. Continue with the line work until both the outside edges meet in the centre, forming a hollow scroll or trumpet.
4. Neaten around the left and right edges (**A** and **B**) with small dots of outline and pipe freehand embroidery from the centre.
5. Left and right shaped scrolls are used to form a decorative pattern.

Hollow line work

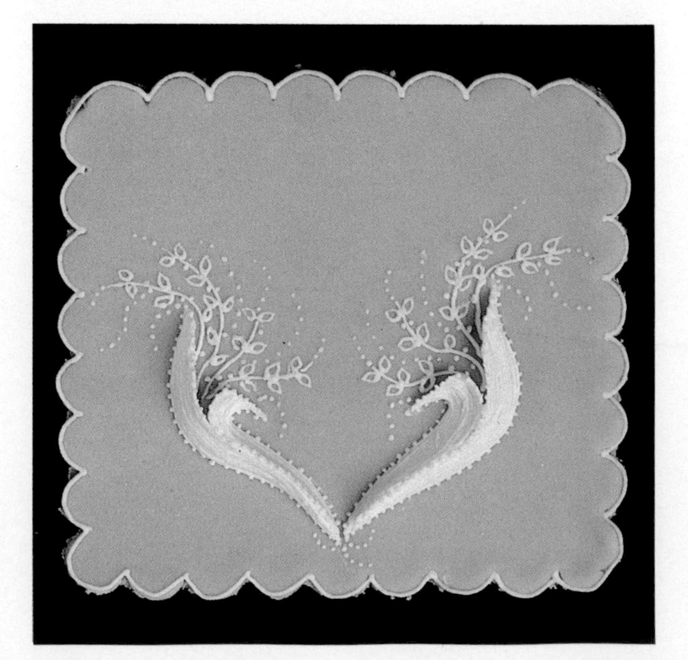

Filigree

The talented decorators of South Africa and Zimbabwe excel in this beautiful art.

For success in this work, great care must be taken when mixing royal icing (see page 16). Once the royal reaches a "soft peak" consistency, place it onto a double thickness of nylon stocking and squeeze to remove any particles of undissolved sugar before filling the piping bag.

1. Trace the design clearly onto greaseproof paper and place it onto a sheet of perspex, glass or laminated board that has had its surface lightly smeared with a white vegetable shortening. Smooth out any creases or bubbles and cover the greaseproof tautly with a piece of waxed paper.
2. Lightly smear the pattern area on the waxed paper with the melted vegetable shortening.
3. Using royal icing and a No. 0 tube, pipe the inside lines of the pattern first, then the outside lines.
4. When the piece is completely dry, pass a warm stream of air from a hair dryer over it, or hold the board in front of a dry heat e.g. a radiator or gas fire, until the vegetable oil melts allowing the filigree to be detached from the waxed paper.

Filigree may also be curved by placing the pattern over suitable shapes such as jars, pipes, or special formers.

Good pressure control is required when piping to ensure even lines. A *touch, lift and place* method is required instead of the decorator trying to "draw" over the pattern with the tube. Accuracy is essential at all times and particularly when executing left and right side pattern pieces.

Once the pieces have been removed rest them on a layer of sponge foam for safety.

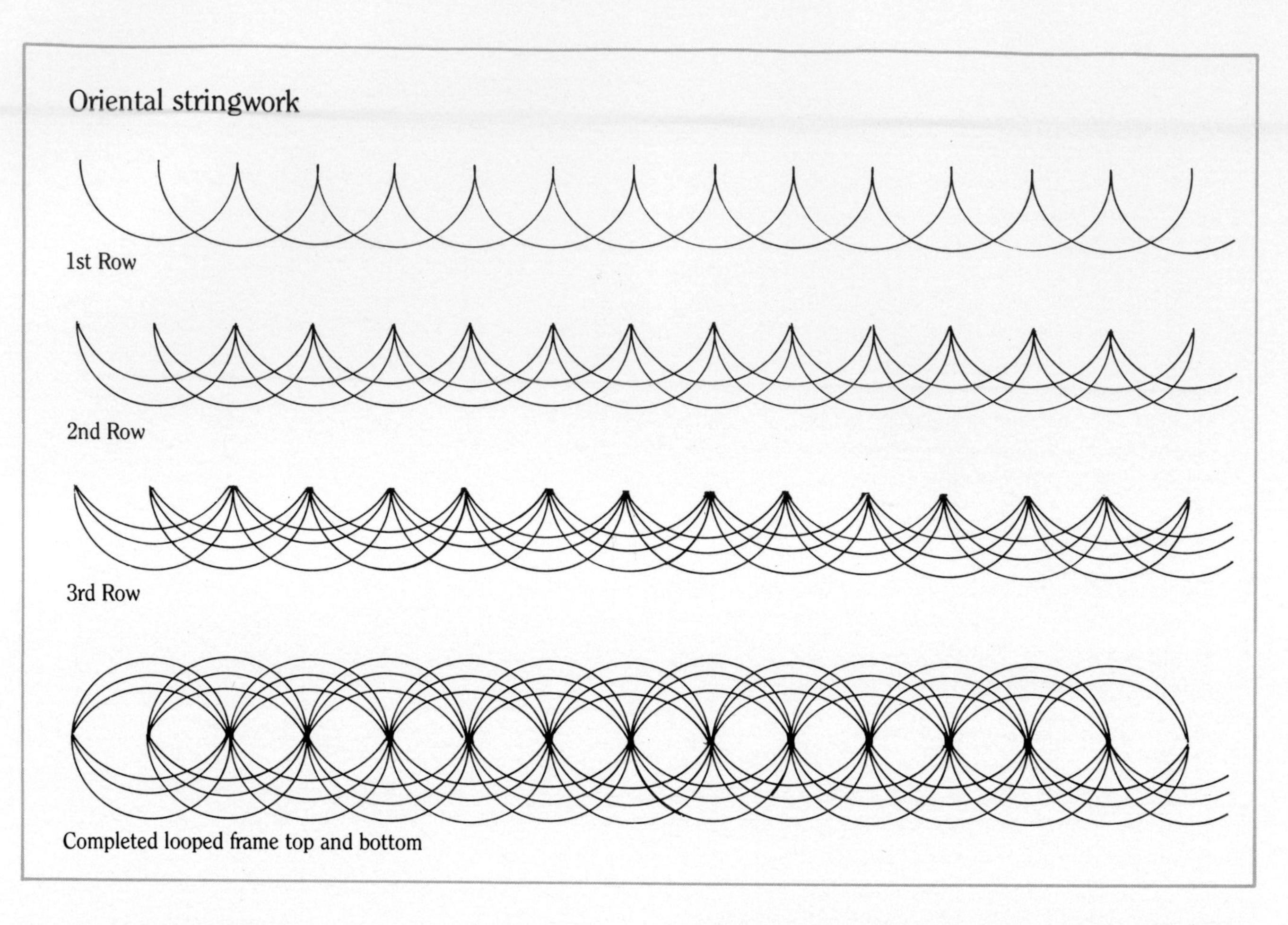

Oriental stringwork

Use the royal icing recipe on page 16.

1. Take a piece of greaseproof paper sufficient in length to just meet around the cake. Along its top edge, evenly mark dots spaced approximately 1.5 cm apart and fitting accurately to the cake's perimeter.
2. Place the template of greaseproof paper around the cake, secure it and mark the dots onto the cover using a No. 0 tube and royal icing. Remove the paper.
3. *1st Row* Pipe drop loops accurately to a pre-determined depth, begin at dot No. 1, miss dot No. 2 and attach to dot No. 3. Now start again on dot No. 2 and pipe a similar loop finishing on dot No 4, thence 3 to 5, 4 to 6 and so on until one row of interlacing loops have been piped completely around the cake.
4. *2nd Row* Pipe a tiny dot at the top of each loop (this will hold the stringwork away from the cake). Repeat the drop loop procedure as before, this time with a shorter depth to the previous scallop.
5. *3rd Row* Repeat this procedure again with a still shorter drop loop, so that the distance between the loops remains the same. Allow to dry.
6. Place a piece of thin foam sponge over the top of a tall firm support of which the diameter is smaller than the cake. Carefully turn the cake so that the top of the cake rests in an upside-down position on top of the foam-covered support.
7. Repeat the drop loop instructions as previously described for rows 1, 2 and 3. Finish off by piping a dot in a contrasting colour where each loop joins. Allow to dry.

Multiple colours may also be used in the loop work for effect. Take care when returning the cake from the support to its original position.

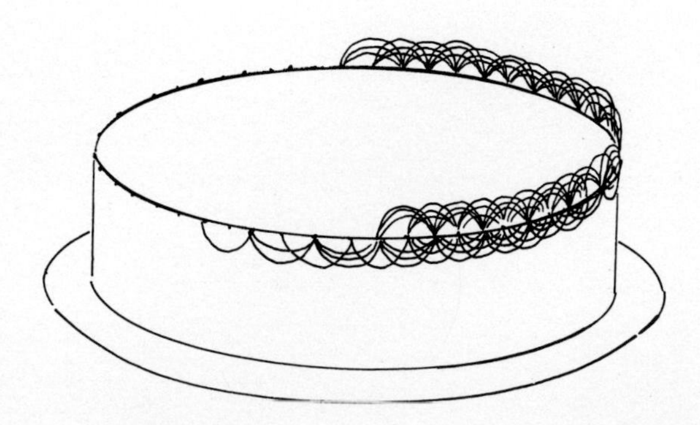

Patchwork appliqué

Patchwork appliqué is almost like working out a jigsaw puzzle in icing, as the pieces are cut individually and re-fitted into the design (see page 124).

The patchwork card on page 6 is similar to one I saw during my visit to South Africa and Zimbabwe. This technique could be adapted in a variety of ways to sugar art work.

1. Trace the pattern and mark it onto the cake or plaque.
2. Colour small pieces of modelling paste or fondant to match those of the design.
3. Mark each section of the pattern by numbering (the lowest numbers are the ones to be applied first).
4. Cut out each section of the pattern individually on a firm paper.
5. Roll the paste or fondant thinly. Begin with the No. 1 pattern piece, place it on the sugar paste or fondant and with a sharp scalpel, cut cleanly around the edge.
6. Once the piece has been cut, it is less confusing to place a piece of clear plastic over the original card (or design) and return each sugar paste pattern into its correct position on the card. Continue, until the original design holds all the pieces.
7. Cover all the cut pattern pieces placed on the plastic to prevent them drying too quickly.
8. Transfer each piece from the plastic into its correct position on the cake or plaque as previously marked after first dampening with water.
9. When every piece has been fitted to complete the design, fill a piping bag with royal icing and a No. 0 tube. Pipe along all the edges with a blanket stitch.

For patterns suitable for patchwork appliqué see page 124.

Appliqué tulle and satin leaves

Tulle and ribbon leaves are suitable for special occasion cakes. These may be used as a spray or as a base border as seen on the *Ballerina Cake*, page 101.

1. Cut a full tulle leaf from the pattern.
2. Cut separately a half leaf (lengthwise) from satin ribbon.
3. Cover a suitable sized piece of dowel or a similar tubular shape tautly with waxed paper.
4. Attach the tulle leaf over the curve and secure it with royal icing dots between the tulle and waxed paper along the outside edges.

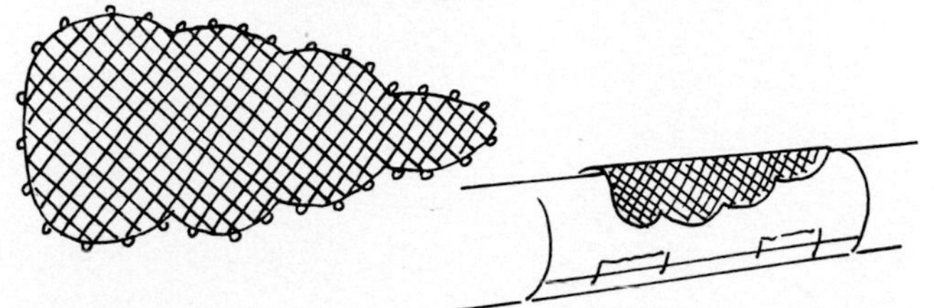

5. Using No. 00 or 0 tube and royal icing, pipe an outline around half the tulle leaf which matches the satin half.
6. Attach the satin ribbon to the wet icing outline. Press to secure.

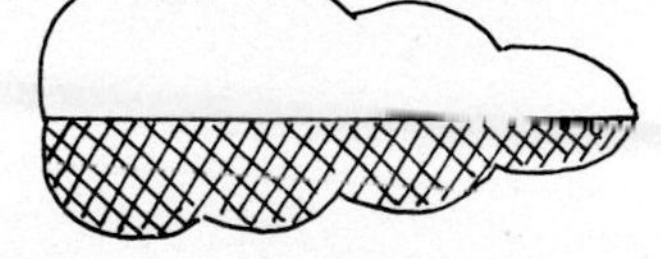

7. Pipe a clean outline completely around the full leaf and down the centre. Then pipe in the veins on both sides of the centre stem.

8. Allow the leaf to dry well before removing from the waxed paper.
9. The sizes of the leaves should vary from large to small.

Side design for Ballerina *cake on page 101.*

Bride and groom — hand moulded mice

The head

1. Begin with a small ball of modelling paste.
2. Shape the nose by pulling to a point and pushing upward with your finger.
3. Make a small cut for the mouth and open slightly. Make a small hole underneath with the end of a paintbrush.
4. Mould a small ball of paste to a petal shape for the ears, press with a ball tool to cup slightly. Attach to the head with water or egg white. Allow to dry completely.
5. Thin some royal icing and colour with caramel. Brush this over the back of the head and ears. Allow to dry for a few minutes then scratch with a pin to produce roughened look of fur.
6. Pipe a dot of royal icing on the tip of the nose.
7. When dry, paint eyes and features with food colouring using a fine brush.

The body

1. Join together with royal icing two balls of paste, the top one smaller than the base ball. Push a toothpick through the centre leaving a small part showing at the top.
2. Allow to dry completely before brushing all over with the thinned caramel-coloured royal icing.
3. Allow to dry for a few minutes before scraping all over with a pin for the fur effect.

Note: The body may also be cut to a pear shape from a styrene ball.

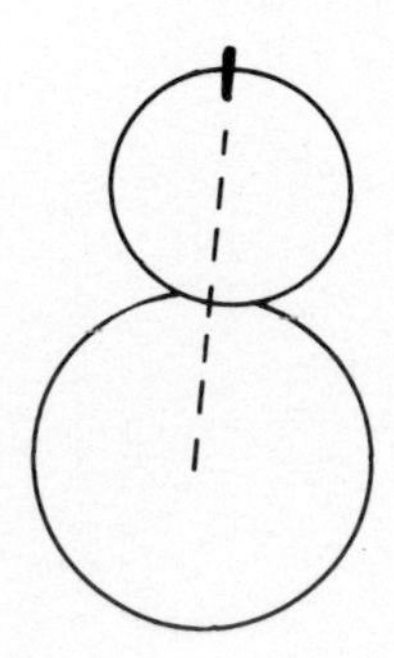

The feet

1. Begin with a small rounded and flattened piece of paste. Cut half way through the centre, then make small cuts for the toes and a short cut at the back for the heels.
2. Shape each of the three toes and push each foot slightly outwards.
3. Brush the feet over with the thinned royal icing as done for the body.

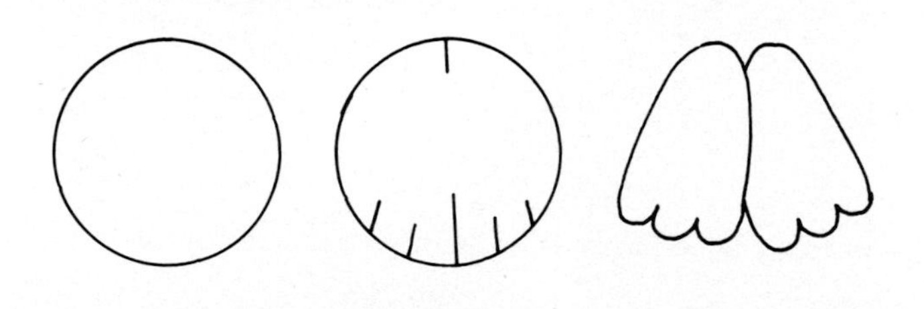

Assembling

1. With royal icing, attach the head to the body, pushing the head onto the toothpick, then attach the body to the feet. Make adjustments for balance by tilting the sections forward or back, then allow to dry completely. It may need to be supported at this stage but when dry should stand by itself.
2. Make a long thin tail. This is easier to attach when the clothes of the mouse have been completed.

Clothes for him

Waistcoat

Cut a front only from thin paste and attach to the body with water or egg white. Paint as desired and pipe royal icing dots for the buttons.

Tails

1. Cut the pattern as a mirror image. Shape each piece around the body and bend back along the dotted line for the jacket lapel. Leave the lower part of the tails open and slightly overlap the top.
2. Pipe small dots for the buttons at the back and front and mould or pipe a small flower for the lapel.

Collar

Cut the collar from thinly rolled paste, fold the top half over on the dotted line and attach around the neck.

Bow tie

1. Roll a thin strip of paste. Fold each end to the centre back and pinch the centre together.
2. Place a small strip over the centre and attach it with royal icing.

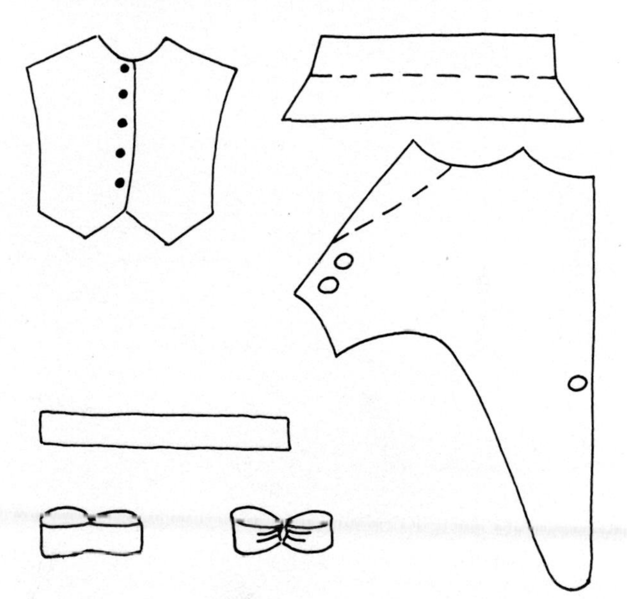

Arms

1. Begin with a log shaped piece of caramel-coloured paste.
2. Cut twice for the fingers, shape each and press them together again.
3. Add a small strip of paste to the wrist for a shirt cuff. Allow to dry completely.

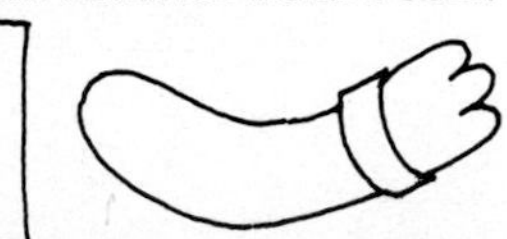

4. Roll the paste and cut and shape the sleeve. Join on the inside of the arm and gather along the top to fit. Crease along the elbow bend, pipe dots for buttons and attach to the body with royal icing. Repeat for other arm.

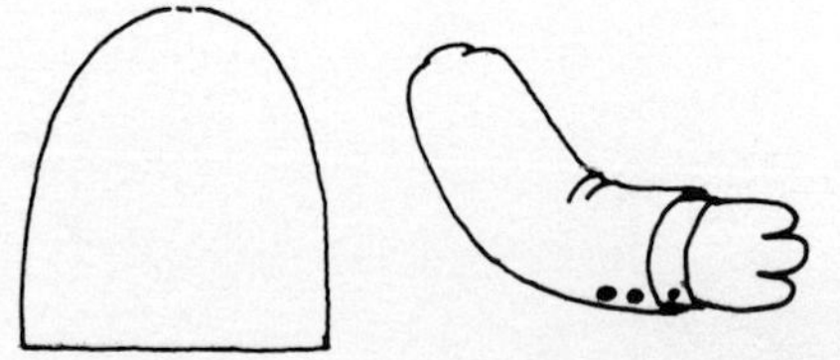

Clothes for her

The dress

1. Frill narrow strips of paste for the petticoat. Start at the bottom, work four rows.
2. Attach a bodice to the front and back, keep the side seams neat.
3. Cut the skirt and gather the waistline. Cut this as one piece allowing an overlap at the back.
4. Neaten the neck edge of the bodice with a small frill.
5. Finish the waist with a band and a bow at the back. Finish the hemline, neck and cuff frills with small piped scallops and dots.

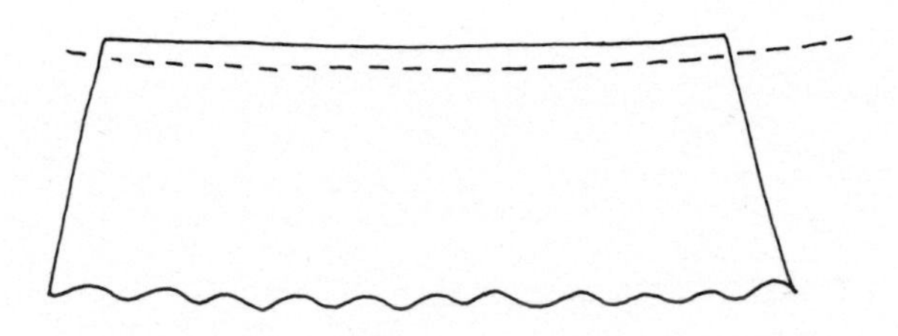

The arms

As previously explained for "him", attaching a frill to each wrist before applying the sleeve.

Veil

1. Measure and cut a piece of fine tulle the desired length. Gather along the dotted lines with a needle and thread. Pull each thread tightly and sew to secure.
2. Attach the veil to the head with royal icing and cover the gathered thread with small piped flowers and leaves.

Moulded figures

These beautiful reproductions have been moulded and dressed by Colleen Willis, one of Zimbabwe's very talented decorators. Colleen uses the Willis moulds for "him" and "her"; if these are unobtainable, similar figure moulds are available in most countries.

This technique is better suited to the experienced decorator, however, the clear instructions and step by step photographs will enthuse those less experienced to make an attempt at figure moulding.

Figure moulding

1. Use a fresh, fast drying, flesh-coloured modelling paste. It is also advisable to use interlocking moulds made of rigid plastic if they are available, as this type of material does not adhere easily to sugar pastes and glues. Consequently, there is less chance of causing damage to your moulds. Grease sparingly all parts of the moulds with white vegetable fat.
2. When moulding human figures for the first time, start with a small piece of paste and practise inserting it into the face mould until all the features can be reproduced perfectly. Then take a larger piece of paste and fill each half of the head and torso mould.
3. Grease a piece of bamboo or a wooden stick with a hole drilled in one end. Insert a wooden toothpick in the piece of bamboo and lay it on the paste in the front half of the mould so that the toothpick reaches almost to the top of the head. The toothpick serves to strengthen the neck and will prevent the head

from breaking off while you are working on the mould, and the piece of bamboo enables you to stand the mould in an upright position until it is dry enough to be handled safely.

4. With your finger, rub a little egg white on the surface of each half of the mould until the paste feels very sticky. Firmly press the two halves together, then separate the moulds immediately and carefully remove the paste figure. While still moist and pliable, adjust the position of the head and facial features to your requirements. Leave to dry for 24 hours.
5. Make the arms and legs by filling each half of the respective moulds with paste, gently rubbing each half with egg white until sticky and pressing the matching halves together. Immediately separate the moulds, position the limbs as required and leave to dry for 24 hours on cotton wool.
6. When dry, with a sharp blade or scalpel, trim off all the flashing (excess paste squeezed out between the two halves of the mould). With great care, additional trimming of ankles, wrists and facial features can also be done at this stage. Carefully remove the pieces of bamboo or dowel and toothpicks.
7. Position legs in an upright position on a small plaque which can later be decorated to fit in with the surroundings. Glue in place and leave to dry (use edible glue described on page 111 and Sticky Gum paste on page 112).

Faces

1. Colour the eyeball white with a cake pencil. Dust cheeks, chin and forehead with rouge or pink powder colour. Apply eye shadow colour of your choice above the woman's eyes and light brown above the man's eyes (non-toxic chalk).
2. With a very fine paintbrush and brown or black food colouring, outline the eyes and paint in a few eyelashes on the outer edge of the top lid. Colour the iris leaving a small section white to represent reflected light. Paint in the eyebrows with short light strokes.
3. Accentuate nostrils and eyelid crease in light brown or grey.
4. Colour lips pink or red.

Clothes

1. Cut shoe uppers out of very thin pieces of paste, glue to feet and cut and shape as required with a scalpel. Mark in seam line, paint laces and add buckles as desired.
2. Basic clothes patterns are supplied for both the man and the woman in the 150 mm and 160 mm sizes respectively (see pages 126 and 127). These can be

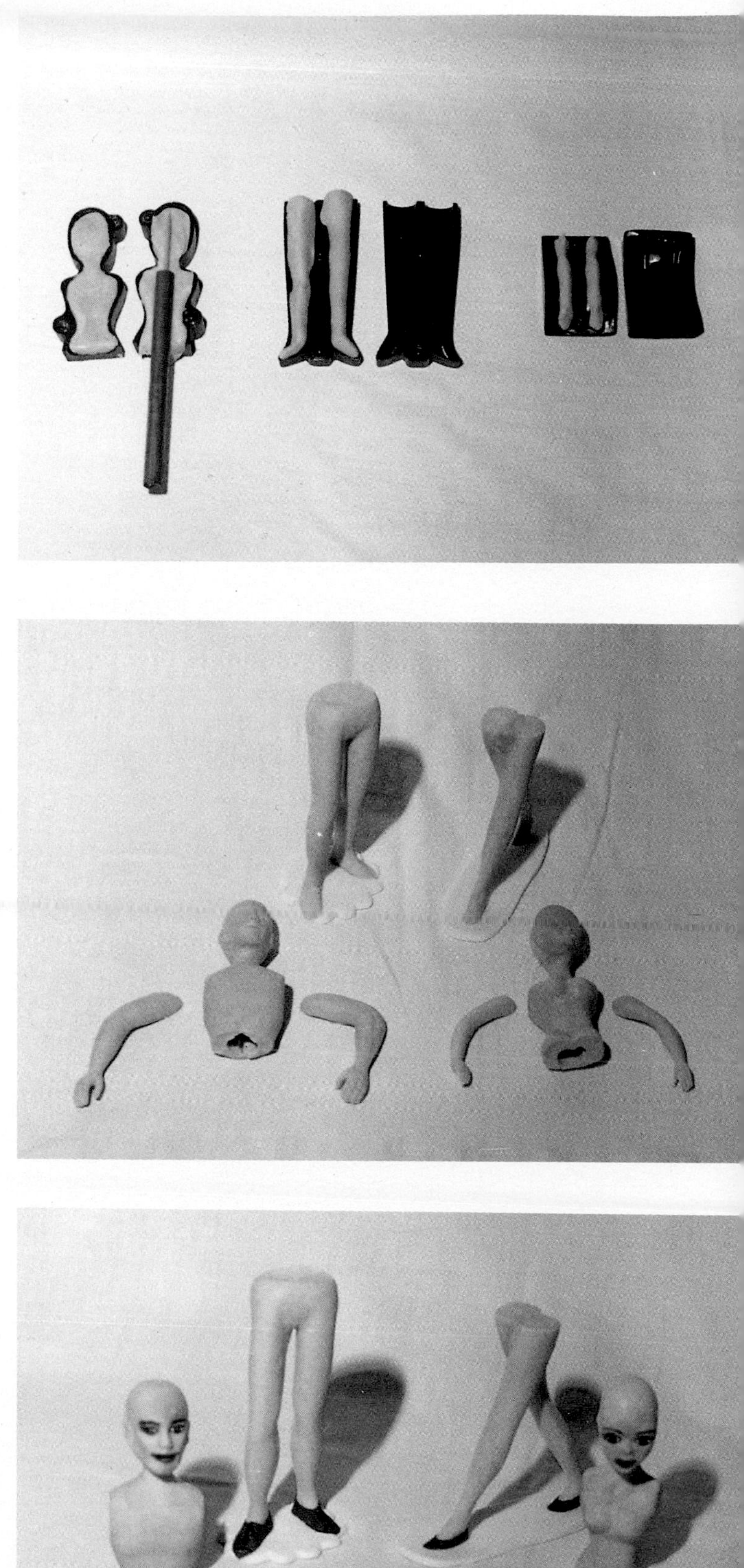

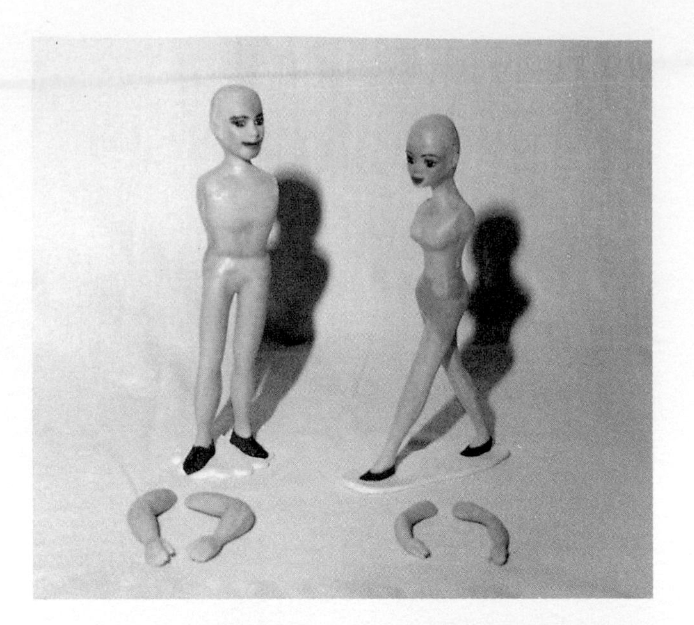

adjusted for larger and smaller dolls accordingly. However, an elementary knowledge of dressmaking is all that is required to enable you to cut your own patterns for clothing your dolls.

3. Do not waste time and effort by dressing your dolls with more layers of clothing than is necessary. For example, if your man is to wear a shirt, a waistcoat and a jacket, you need only dress him with that part of the shirt that will show, the front of the waistcoat and the whole of the jacket. To incorporate all of the shirt and the back of the waistcoat would add unnecessary bulk and give a rather overweight appearance to the final figure. The same rule of thumb applies to the woman.
4. Whether the top half or the bottom half of the body is to be dressed first depends entirely on the style of dress selected. As a general rule, dress your doll in the same order as you would dress if you were wearing the same attire. In dressing your doll do not be too liberal in your use of glue/egg white. Glue should only be applied to the edges of each piece of clothing and only to those edges which need to be glued in place. Before starting to dress your doll, glue the head and torso to the legs and blend in the join with a small quantity of modelling paste. Some, however, may prefer to leave this operation to a later stage when the doll is partially clothed.
5. Do not dress or position the arms until the rest of the doll has been clothed. Dress each arm and before the sleeve is dry, carefully glue it in position on the doll using a small ball of modelling paste and a little egg white. Collars and frills which fall over the shoulder line should be added after the arms are in position. Neaten the shoulder seams and leave to dry.
6. When the arms are firmly in position, add finishing touches such as a bow tie, a necklace, rings, earrings, bracelets and paint finger nails, etc. These finishing touches can be added in royal icing or paste — whichever is the most suitable medium for the item required.

Hair

1. The hair is executed in royal icing and can be done by either using a very fine writing nozzle and suitably coloured royal icing, and piping the hair into the desired style; or using the painting-in-icing technique, colour and style your doll's hair with a paintbrush and liquid food colouring.
2. The latter technique has been used on the dolls illustrated because it normally results in a softer hair style and more natural colouring than the former technique.

CAKES

Preparation of baking pans

Care in the paper lining of cake tins will save time in packing the cake prior to covering with almond paste and fondant. Multiple layers of brown paper and greaseproof paper are required for this purpose. Approximately two sheets of brown and three of greaseproof will be necessary. Directions for lining the square, oval and round cake pans, see page 60.

Where cake pans are of shapes difficult to paper-line, spray the inside of the tin well with a non stick cooking spray. Trace out the shape of the base of the tin onto the brown and greaseproof paper as directed for the oval and round cakes (see diagram, page 60). Paper-line the base only, before placing the fruit mixture into the pan. Fold several thicknesses of paper into a strip, sufficient in length to go completely around the outside of the tin plus an overlap and tie securely. This will prevent heat penetration drying the cake during the cooking period.

There are many different shapes and sizes of cake tins available and the decorator should assess the cost of hiring these tins against the value of owning them. Many cake decorators' supply shops have a hiring service which could prove beneficial to the decorator requiring a particular shape for one special occasion.

When baking tiered cakes, it is most important that all the pans are identical in shape and proportionate in size, unless the creative style of the cakes are such that they are specifically meant to differ from the conventional.

Square cake

1. Place multiple layers of brown paper and greaseproof paper on the table.
2. Mark the base of the cake pan, then measure a 10 cm border all around, as illustrated on page 60.
3. Cut the paper along the dotted lines.
4. Crease along inside lines and fold the paper, to make a box lining.
5. Place inside the tin.

Oval or round cake

1. Mark the base of the tin on the paper.
2. Cut a separate strip of paper 12 cm wide and the length equal to the circumference of the tin plus an overlap.
3. Rule a line 2 cm from the base of the paper, along the entire length.
4. Make cuts with a pair of scissors along this margin at regular intervals and fold along this line.
5. Insert the paper strip into the pan with the slashed band resting on the base of the tin.
6. Place the base lining over this to secure.

Cake preparation

Great care must be taken in the early preparation of the cake as the trimming, packing and covering is the foundation for the future decorations.

Remove the paper from the cake, then level and trim the cake to ensure that it is symmetrical.

Most cakes are turned bottom-up to decorate, as this provides a flat area which allows more scope for design. However, this is purely a matter of personal choice for the decorator; sometimes the natural fall from the top of the cake is preferred, according to the style selected (see *Mothers Day Cake*, page 47).

Place the cake on a sheet of greaseproof paper. Pack any fruit holes or paper creases with almond or marzipan paste or fondant. Use a small table knife (or palette knife) to press the paste firmly into each hole or crevice, until the packing is smooth and level with the surface. No bumps should be visible. Once the packing has been completed, brush the entire surface *lightly* with brandy or heated apricot purée (see page 108).

Beautiful Vanda orchids decorate this special occasion cake (see page 86).

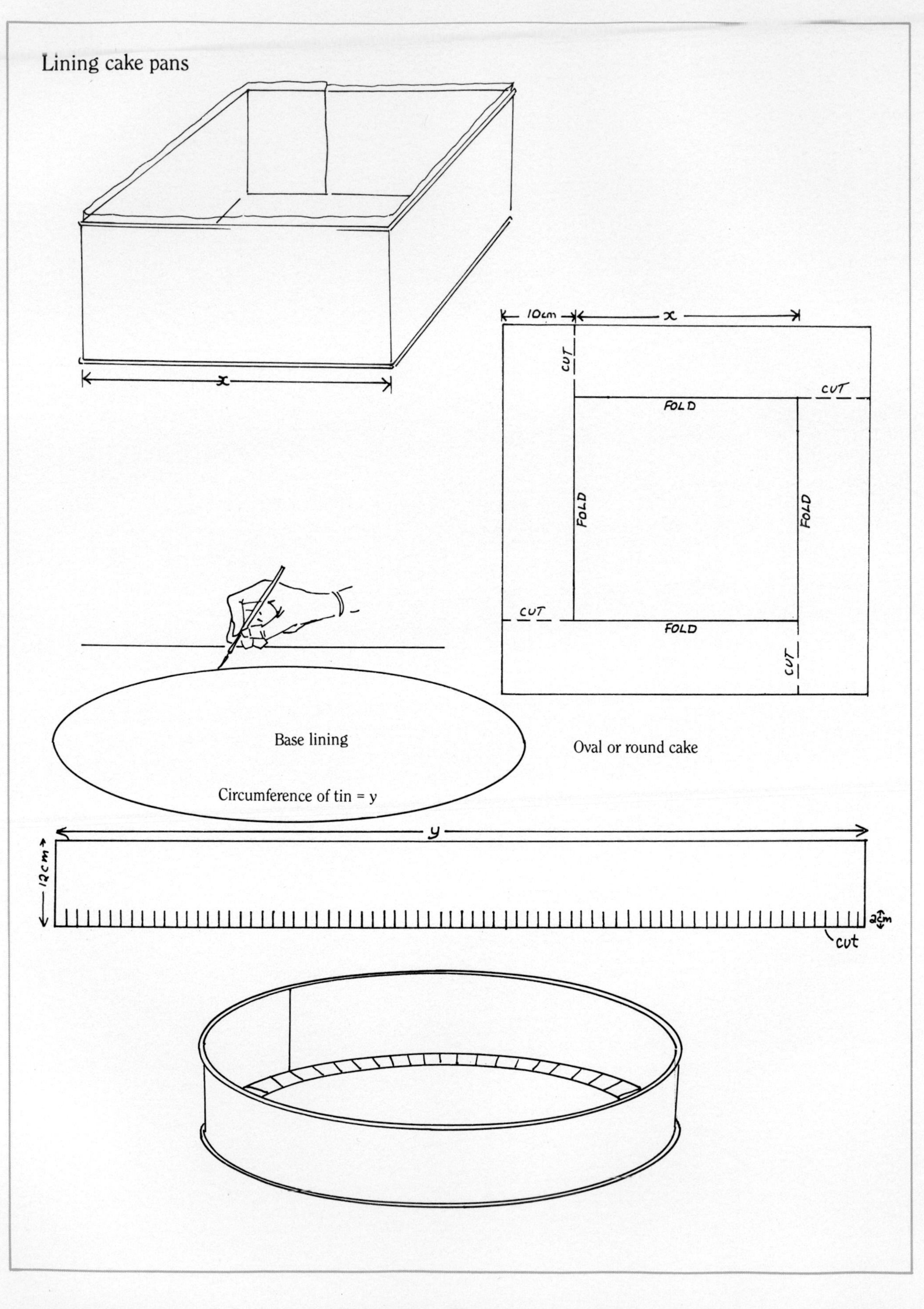
Lining cake pans
x
10cm
x
CUT
CUT
FOLD
FOLD
FOLD
CUT
FOLD
CUT
Base lining
Circumference of tin = y
Oval or round cake
y
12cm
2cm
cut

The cake is now ready for its covering of almond paste. (Marzipan paste may be used as an alternative. Marzipan meal is much cheaper than ground almonds.)

Covering the cake with almond paste

Brush all crumbs away from the working area. Dust icing sugar on a board, marble slab, or laminated surface.

Knead the paste well before rolling it out to a size sufficient to cover the cake. Leave as much thickness in the paste as possible. (By rolling it large and thin, there is too much waste in the off cuts and the cover is not as good).

Once rolled, transfer the paste to the cake with the aid of a rolling pin. Using the palms of the hands or a smoother, work the paste firmly over the top first before working the sides, to prevent trapping air pockets between the cake and the cover. Trim the excess paste away from the base with a sharp knife. Cut cleanly, holding the knife vertically and flush with the surface.

This is a quicker method of applying the undercover than pasting the sides separately with almond paste before attaching the top section. Uncooked almond paste is short in texture and lacks pliability. Due to this, cracks sometimes appear in the surface. Should this happen, pinch the crack together and rub it gently with the palm of the hand until an even surface has been regained.

Allow the almond covering to dry for approximately 2 days to ensure that the oil from the almonds will not penetrate and discolour the plastic icing.

When using marzipan paste, the drying time may be reduced to 12 hours.

Cake covering

Plastic icing or fondant (see page 108)

Knead the plastic icing until it is smooth and pliable.

If the icing is to be coloured, do it in daylight and not by night under electric lights, as this often creates a wrong impression as to the depth of colour required. When the colour is viewed in daylight, the decorator is often disappointed because it is too heavy.

Make sure the working area is clear of all cake crumbs then lightly brush the surface of the almond paste cover with brandy or warmed apricot purée (see page 108).

Roll out the plastic icing on a smooth surface dusted with cornflour or icing sugar until it is large enough to cover the cake. Do not roll the plastic icing too thin or it will provide a poor cover, which will show any bumps or depressions that may already be in the almond covering.

Transfer the plastic icing to the cake with the aid of a rolling pin. Should air bubbles appear in the fondant, prick these immediately with a fine needle and rub gently with the fingers to exude the air.

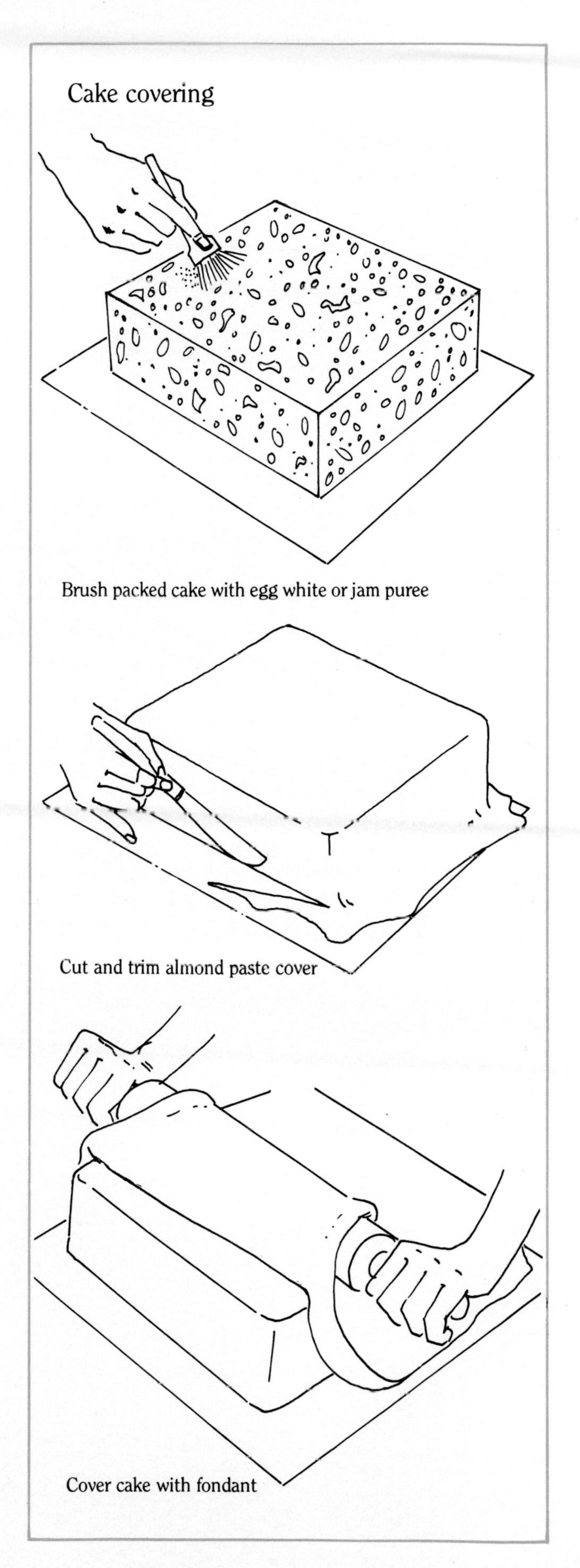

Cake covering

Brush packed cake with egg white or jam puree

Cut and trim almond paste cover

Cover cake with fondant

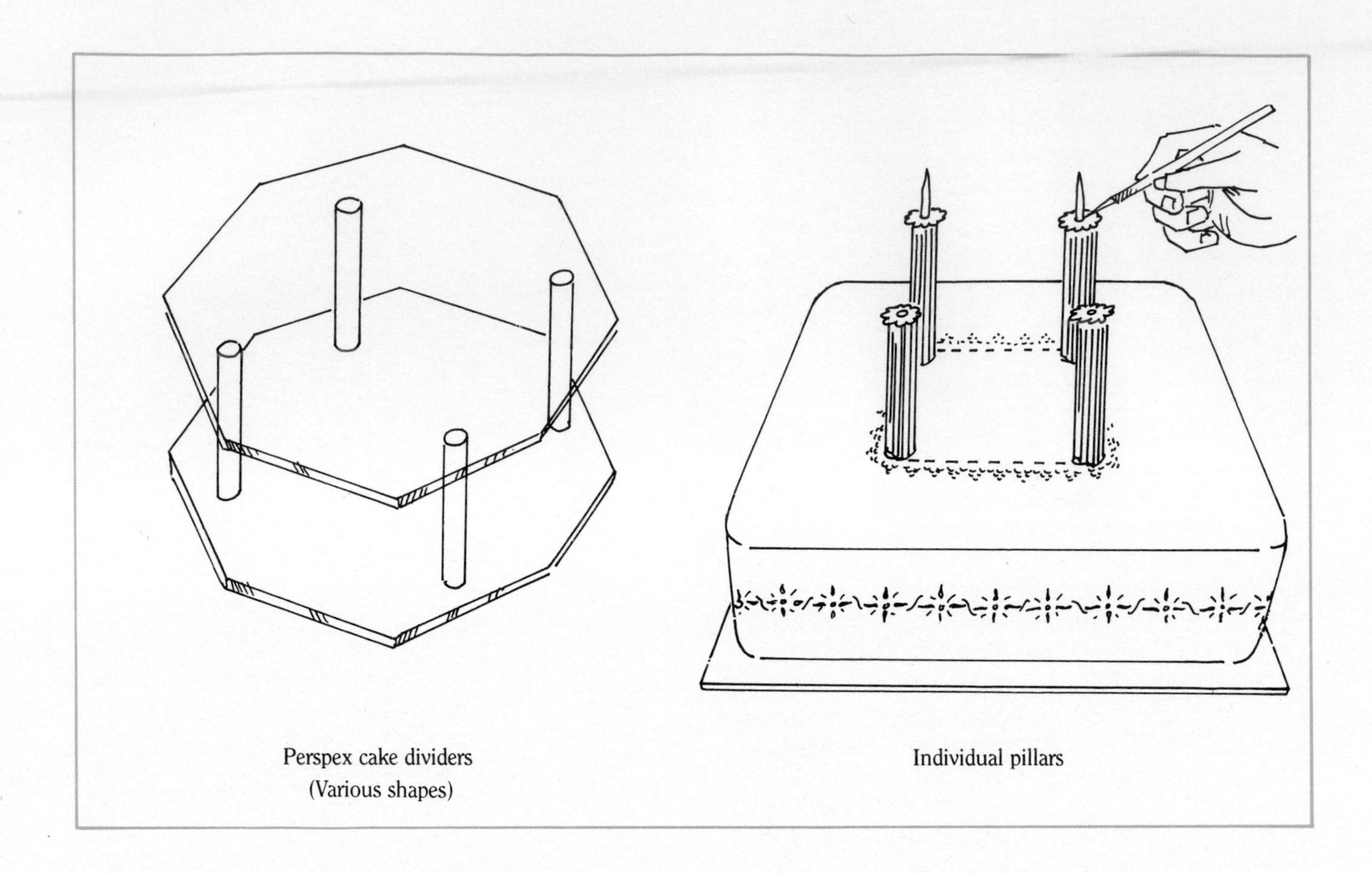

Perspex cake dividers
(Various shapes)

Individual pillars

Now rub over the surface of the fondant using the palms of the hand or smoothers, making sure the top is adhered before working on the sides. This will ensure that air pockets have not been trapped between the two covers.

Do not over-work the plastic icing by excessive rubbing, otherwise the icing will be rubbed thin over the top edges and corners.

With a sharp knife trim around the base of the cake, then cut the greaseproof paper upon which the cake stands level with the plastic icing. The greaseproof paper left under the cake will prevent the acid from the fruit having an effect on the paper covering the base board.

Pillars on tiered cakes

Pillars are used to support and divide the upper tiers of the cake. Tier boards are covered top and bottom with the covering of choice.

Manufactured pillars may not always be of uniform height, therefore it is essential to check that they are all level before buying. There are a variety of different materials such as plastic, perspex, sugar, and metal from which to make a choice.

Many pillars are already attached to a common base, making it easy for the decorator to place these evenly on the cake without bother.

If single pillars are to be used, measure the exact size of the supporting cake on a piece of greaseproof paper and mark it with pencil where the pillars are to be placed. Place the greaseproof paper over the base cake and mark with a probe or skewer the centre of each pillar.

Remove the pattern and insert a wooden skewer or sate stick into each marked position, placing the skewer so that the flat end rests on the base board of the cake.

Place the pillar over each skewer and mark the skewer with a pencil exactly level with the top of each pillar. Remove the pillars and skewers after noting each individual position. Cut each skewer at the pencil line and replace it into its original position. Subsequent tiers are treated in the same manner.

Offset wedding cake featuring sprays of moulded roses and filigree lace trimmed base uses short 4 cm plastic pillars to separate layers.

HAND-MOULDED FLOWERS & FOLIAGE

MOULDED FLOWERS

This must surely be one of the most fascinating and interesting techniques of sugar work.

Patience is the name of the game, for that is what it takes to reach a standard where even the bees and Mother Nature may be fooled.

Use your garden as a friend, study closely the shape and detail of each flower and leaf. You will be surprised how much more you will learn when you study and not just look.

Learn to make your own patterns from nature by selecting 2 or 3 of the best blooms from the same plant. Use one for a pattern and carefully remove the petals with a sharp scalpel. Keep the others fresh in water to have for reference when you make up a sample flower.

Carefully place each of the removed petals onto a piece of white paper in the same order as they appeared on the original flower. Should variation of shape occur, it will be necessary to trace around each petal and make a note of the number of rows and the number of stamens to the flower.

If the multiple petals are the same size and shape, only trace around one of the petals for a pattern. Make a note of the number of petals required and how the petals are arranged, particularly where there is more than one row. Special note should be made as to the shape of buds, leaves and calyx.

Patterns should be clearly marked for easy recognition. Try to make up a sample of the flower while it is in bloom and at its prime. These samples are an excellent reference during the period that the flower is out of season.

Do not be afraid to tint and shade your work. Build up from the paler to the deeper tonings; make your work look alive and interesting.

Important points for success when moulding

1. Use pliable and elastic modelling paste.
2. Finely texture petals and leaves.
3. Smooth edges with fingers or tool to avoid roughness or cracks.
4. Take care with colour, tinting and shading.
5. Take care when assembling.
6. Use wire of suitable strength to hold the flower or leaves.

Anthurium

A lily-like flower with a high gloss appearance. Colours are bright red, orange-red, white and pink.

Central spadix

1. Take a piece of firm wire and insert it into a cone of yellow modelling paste, 5 cm long. Allow the spadix to fall to a slight natural curve. Leave to dry.
2. Mix a little semolina polenta or gelatine with some powdered buttercup yellow chalk. Dampen the spadix with water and roll well into the selected mixture to create the impression of pollen.

Flower

1. Thinly roll a piece of modelling paste and using a cutter or pattern cut the shape from it. Vein with a veiner, or over a deeply grooved foam tray onto which the outline has been marked and the internal vein system deeply indented with the handle of a paintbrush. (Thanks to Mavis Mephan for this last hint.) Ball tool the edge.

Driftwood setting for Anthuriums, Honeysuckle, Gypsophila, Ribbon grass, Ivy and Privet leaves.

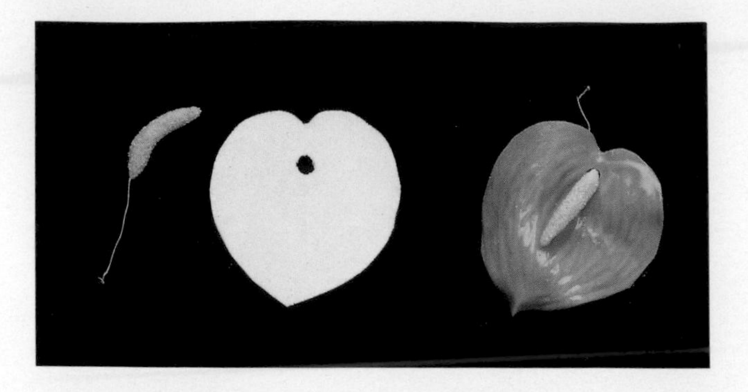

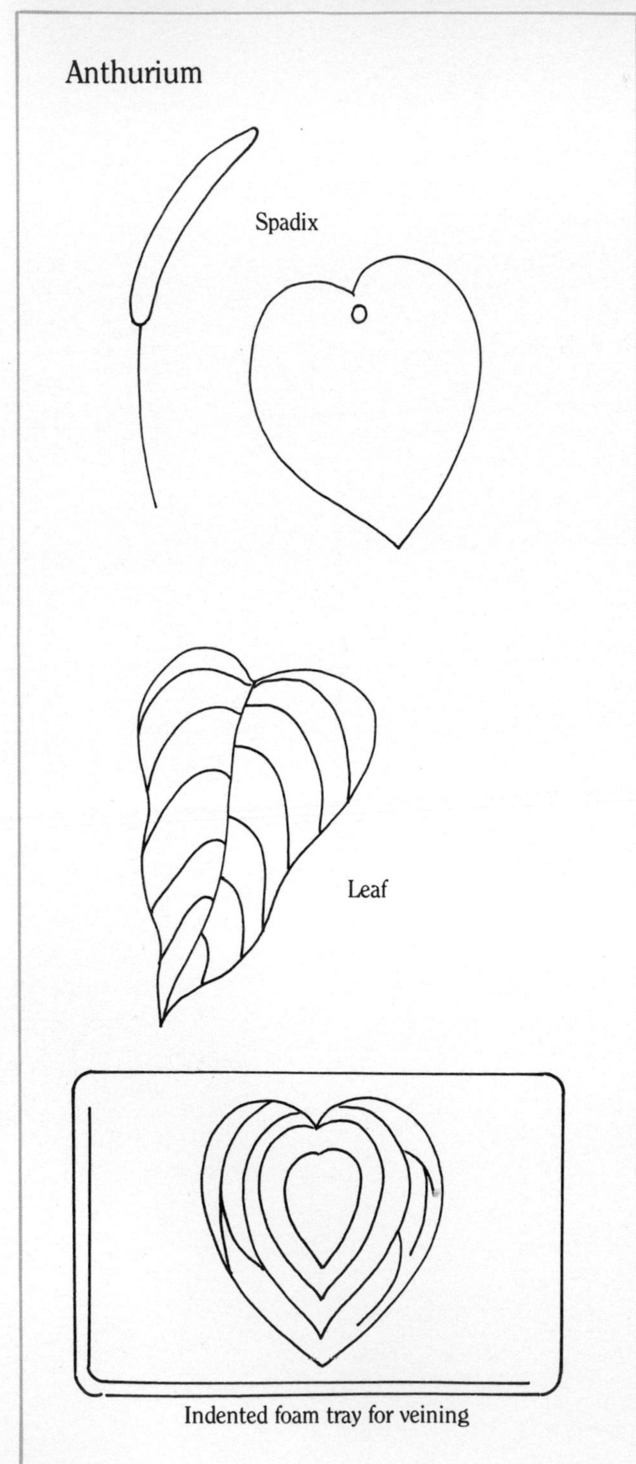

Indented foam tray for veining

2. Make a small hole 5 mm from the heart centre then set the flower to dry in a tray of cornflour or shaped over a cottonwool ball.
3. When dry, chalk dust or paint with food colour the desired shade.
4. Brush a little of the chalk colour to the base of the spadix and insert the wire through the hole until the centre touches the flower. Use royal icing to join both together; allow to dry before brushing the flower over with an edible glaze (see page 112).

Bougainvillea

This beautiful climber blooms in vibrant colours of red, purple, magenta, cerise, burnt orange, white and pink.

The three central spines which appear as stamens are the flower, and the petal to which each is attached is the bract.

Central spikes (flower)

1. The length of each spike is approximately ⅔ the length of the bract.
2. Take a piece of fine wire and taper a thin sausage of yellow modelling paste over it in accordance to the length of the bract.
3. Pinch 5 grooves vertically around this sausage with a pair of flat tipped tweezers, then flatten the top by pinching a small circular ridge and cut to make 5 equal sections of the flower.
4. Round each petal and pinch lightly between the fingers to form the flower.
5. Paint the spike below the yellow flower the same colour as the outside bracts and allow to dry thoroughly.

Bracts (or petals)

1. Roll out the modelling paste thinly and cut 3 bracts, using either a pattern or cutter. Cover two while working on one to prevent drying. Fold the bract in half and mark a centre ridge, open the bract keeping the ridge topside.

2. Attach the bract to the dried central spike (flower) by dampening the base of the central ridge of the bract. Pinch well at the low edge and turn the broad part of the petal back slightly to allow the three bracts, when completed, to fit neatly together.
3. Paint fine lacey veins onto each bract with a 00 brush in a deeper shade of food colouring. Flowers vary in size from small medium to large.

To assemble

Grade the sizes and tape flowers and leaves together as a spray.

Double bouvardia

This very dainty flower grows in a variety of colours which complements any spray where "filler flowers" are required.

1. Shape a hollow cone from a small piece of modelling paste and cut the top into 4 equal sections. Cut each section using a pair of sharp scissors, into semi-pointed petals. Smooth the cut edge of each petal.
2. Lightly dampen the centre and insert a piece of fine wire, knotted. Secure it firmly in the base of the flower. Using a small ball tool, place it into the centre of the flower, cupping the petals around it to form a semi-opened flower. Allow this to dry thoroughly.
3. Now shape a hollow longish cone of paste, cut the top edge into 4 as previously instructed. While holding each petal between the fingers to smooth and soften the edges, stretch a little to lengthen them before turning slightly back and away from the centre. Lightly dampen the base of the wired flower and insert this through the flower cone until the section rests compactly with its petals alternating with those below. Allow to dry before colouring with chalk or liquid food colouring.
4. Paint a small shading of green to the base of each flower where it tapers to the wire.

Double bouvardia

Buds

Tiny balls of paste tapered over a fine wire.

The vibrant Bougainvillea make a spectacular show used as sprays for cake or plaque arrangements.

Sasanqua camellia

1. Take a cluster of yellow stamens, cut them approximately 1¼ cm in length, bind together with a fine wire then tape to a medium wire with florist tape.
2. Using a pale pink modelling paste roll a small log-sized piece and insert a short length of fine wire, dampened at one end, into approximately ⅓ the length of the finished petal.
3. Roll the paste to the left and right of the centre wire until the paste is fine enough to cut the pattern. Make sure the wire is in the centre of the pattern before cutting cleanly around the edge with a sharp scalpel.
4. Smooth with your fingertips or tool the cut edge before softly fluting. Vein lightly and drape over a cotton wool ball to obtain a soft curve.
5. Repeat this process until 4 large petals and 4 small petals have been made for each flower. Allow all petals to dry thoroughly before assembling.

To assemble

1. Take the 4 small petals and place them into position at the base of the stamen cluster. Place the remaining 4 large petals below the spaces of the first row. Hold all wires together firmly and tape together.
2. Shade the flower with petal dust.

Calyx

1. Using a rounded 5-petal cutter, roll out a piece of green paste and cut out the calyx.
2. Press a ball tool into each of the 5 petals before dampening the centre with water and inserting the wire stem of the flower through. Attach firmly to the back of the flower.

Leaf

Cut as pattern, chalk dust when dry.

Christmas bells

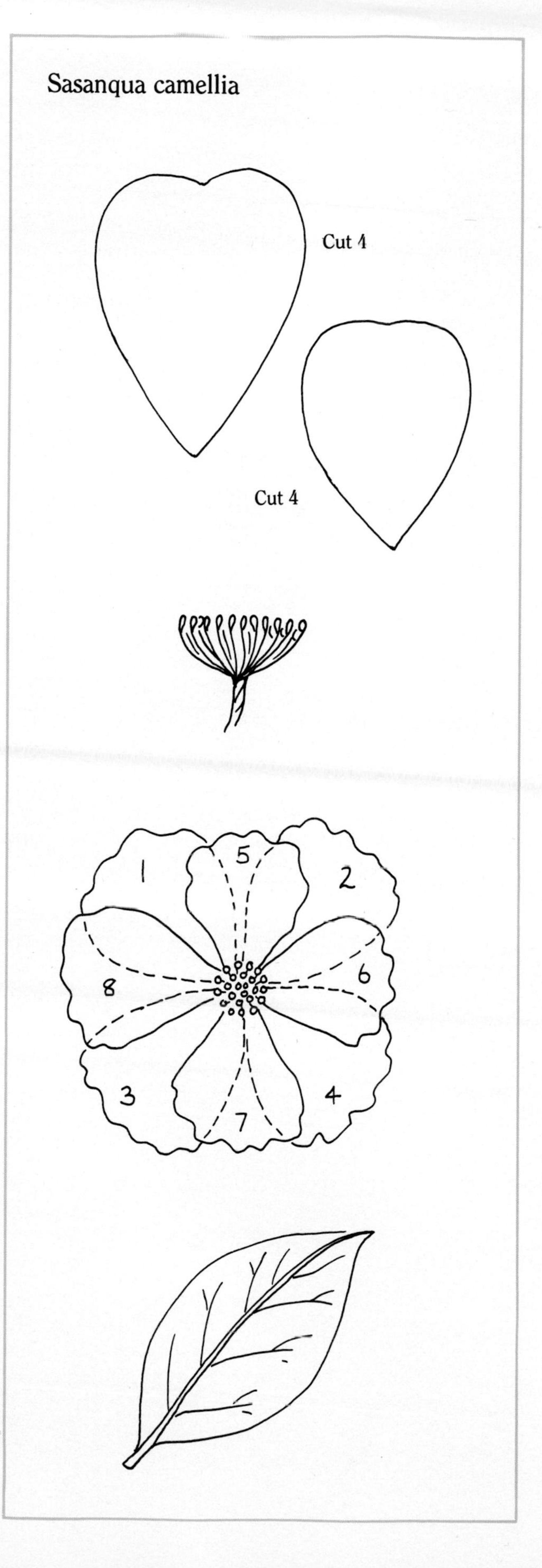

Christmas bells

1. Hollow-cone a small log-shaped piece of buttercup yellow modelling paste.
2. Cut 6 equal portions approximately 4 mm deep and cut each side to a softly pointed petal.
3. Press each petal lightly between the thumb and index fingers and turn back slightly to give a more natural look.
4. Moisten the internal base of the flower with water and insert a short length of medium strength wire to which 7 yellow stamens have been taped, one longer than the others. Allow to dry.
5. Chalk dust the outside of the bell, or paint with pillar box red food colouring, leaving a yellow area at the tip of the petals into which the red is merged in an irregular blending.
6. A pale green tip to each petal, very minutely applied, and the long stamen touched with green, completes this colourful flower.

Bud

1. The bud is an elongated piece of paste, thicker at the top and tapering at the base, over a dampened piece of wire. Mark in the 6 unopened petals at the top. Allow to dry.
2. Chalk dust or paint the bud with the same colour as the flower, leaving a small space at the tip of the bud to colour green. Vary the size of the buds.

Note: If using liquid colour, allow the pillar box red to dry before applying the green, otherwise it will run together, making a brown.

Leaf

This is a long blade shape.

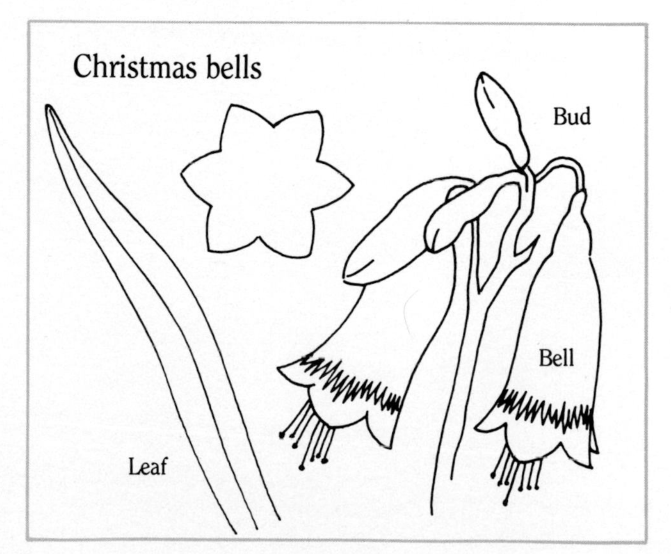

Christmas bush

1. Remove the tip of the stamen and cut the cotton stem into 5 short lengths. Colour the tips of the cotton a deep red, allowing the paler cotton base to be seen. Tape these to a wire with florist tape.
2. Using a small pea-sized piece of pale pink or white modelling paste, insert a flower stick (or brush handle) and hollow-cone it out. Cut the cup into 5 equal sections for the petals.
3. Semi-point each petal by cutting with a small pair of scissors.
4. Take each petal individually between the cushion of the thumb and forefinger. Press gently to soften cut edge. At the same time, stretch each petal a little and turn back slightly.
5. Dampen the centre of the flower before inserting the wire and stamens. Attach the paste to the wire.
6. When dry, chalk dust with red, or paint with liquid red food colouring. Leave the centre of the flower a little paler than the petals.

Buds

These have a round top, they are tapered slightly to the base and attached to wire.

Leaves

These are elongated, varying in size. Wire may be inserted into a sausage shape before rolling and cutting.

Christmas bush

Chrysanthemum

Three sized daisy cutters are required. Small, medium and large (see diagrams on page 72).

Bud

1. Hook a piece of 0.018 inch wire at right angles, and insert it into a piece of modelling paste. Press the base of the paste flat and the top as a dome.

Chrysanthemum

2. Using a small pair of sharp-pointed scissors, cut the outside petals around the bud first, then the inner petals, until the dome of paste is completely covered with tiny petals all over.
3. Flatten the petals, re-shape the dome and allow to thoroughly dry before attaching the next rows of flower petals.

Petals

1. Using the smallest daisy cutter cut 2 layers from thinly rolled paste. Cover one while working on the other.
2. Cut each of the 8 petals into two. Press a tapered tool or knitting needle into each half petal to make a groove. Pinch the top of each petal to form a point.
3. Dampen the back of the bud and insert the wire through the centre of the petal layer.
4. Press the petals over and around the bud.
5. Repeat with the second layer of petals, stretching each petal to make it a little longer than the previous row.
6. Using the next sized cutter, cut 2 layers. Cover one while working on the other.
7. Cut each petal into 2 (8 petals). Using a tapered tool, press and broaden each petal, stretch slightly and pinch the tips. Attach to the bud as previously directed.
8. Repeat this method with the second layer. *Do not* pinch the tip of the petals. Stretch these petals a little longer than the previous row. Attach in the same way.
9. Using the largest cutter, continue in the same manner. Leave a little more thickness in the paste before cutting in order that the petals may be rolled a little broader and stretched a little longer than the previous rows. Attach in the same way. Allow to dry.

A beautiful spray of Chrysanthemums and Wild Violets

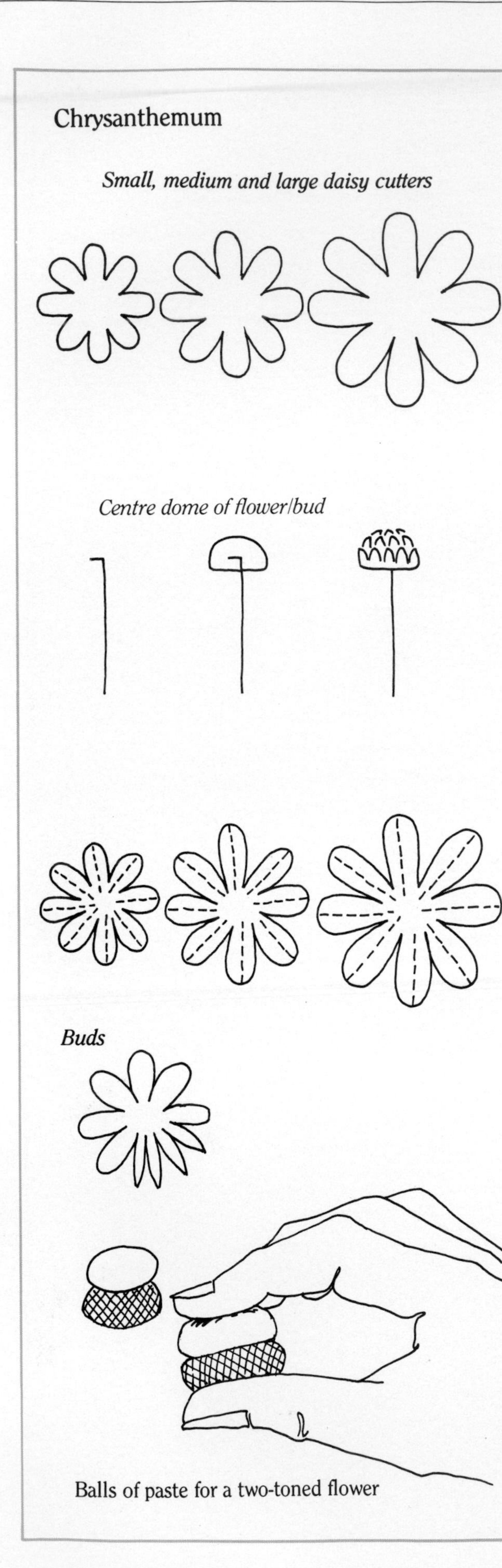

Calyx

Hollow-cone and cut a piece of green modelling paste into 5 equal sections. Cut 5 pointed tops. Insert the wired flower through the calyx and attach firmly to the flower after dampening with a little water.

Leaves

1. These may be cut from natural leaves of various sizes.
2. Roll out the paste thinly, place the leaf on top of the paste and roll over the leaf lightly with a small rolling pin. Cut around the outline implanted in the paste with a small sharp scalpel. Tool around the outer edge, shape and allow to dry before chalk dusting.

Buds

These are made in various sizes as previously instructed, using only one layer of petals and a calyx. To produce a two-toned flower, press 2 balls of colour together, e.g. yellow and copper tone. Roll them out thinly before cutting with the petal daisy cutter.

Cotoneaster

1. Roll pea-sized pieces of red modelling paste and insert a piece of fine knotted wire through the centre. Make 10-12 for each berry cluster. Allow to dry.
2. Brush over the surface of each berry with gum arabic solution to produce a glaze (see page 111).
3. When dry, pipe one black royal icing dot in the centre of the berry to cover the wire and a row of five dots close to the centre one.
4. Cluster the berries together and tape the stems with florist tape.

Leaves

Green modelling paste, wired, rolled, cut and veined. Several are grouped together below the berry clusters and taped to the stem. Cotoneaster berries also grow in orange and crimson colours.

Boronia — elatior

1. Take a small pea-sized piece of modelling paste. Hollow-cone it out, then cut it to form four equal sections.
2. Cut each section into a semi-pointed petal and insert a piece of fine wire (hooked or knotted) through to the base of the cone and secure firmly into the paste.
3. Soften the petal edges by smoothing each one lightly with the fingertips.
4. Cup some of the flowers to give a roundish shape by pressing a small ball tool lightly into each petal. Open others, to indicate the older and more developed growth by turning the petals back and away from the centre.

Buds

1. These are made from a round ball of paste, attached to wire and marked into four sections at the top.
2. When the flowers and buds are dry, colour with pink chalk, or liquid colour diluted with water or pure alcohol. Pipe a pale green stamen in the centre of each flower.

Leaves

These are quite tiny. Roll a small log of green paste and insert a fine damp wire. Roll left and right of the wire until the paste is thin enough to cut the leaf. Vein and allow to dry.

To assemble

Take a group of three buds and tape them together to a central wire. Add the flowers and leaves, beginning with the smallest and finishing with the largest, according to the size spray required.

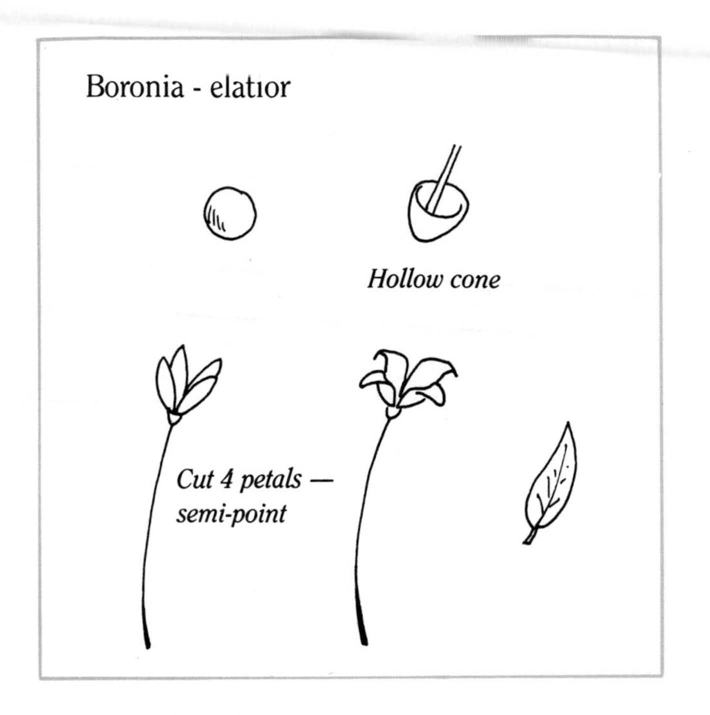

Flannel flower

This native Australian and New Zealand plant has creamy-white, felt-like flowers with greyish foliage.

In a container, colour approximately ¼ cup of caster sugar, by adding a little leaf green, yellow and brown liquid colouring. Hand work the colours through the sugar until the desired shade of grey-green is obtained. Allow the sugar to dry.

Flower centre

1. Take a small piece of grey-green modelling paste, attach it to a dampened hooked wire (see diagram page 74). Firm it securely around the wire and form a domed top, with a flattish base.
2. Allow to dry, then dip it into a solution of egg white and water, then into the coloured sugar. Allow to fully dry and shake off any excess sugar. This forms the centre of the flower.

Gypsophila

The size of these flowers vary from very small to approximately 1.5 cm in diameter.

1. Using a flower stick tool, or the handle of a paintbrush, hollow out a pea-sized piece of white sugar paste until a small cone results.
2. Cut the hollowed cone into 5 equal petals. Cut the corners from each section and nip a ∨ in the centre top of each petal.
3. Insert a 5-edged umbrella tool into the centre of the flower and press to groove each petal.
4. Dampen the base of the flower, insert a piece of fine covered knotted or hooked wire and secure the flower firmly. (or insert a pearl stamen).
5. Take each petal, one at a time between the thumb and forefinger and bend it slightly away from the centre of the flower.
6. Brush a little pale yellow-green colour into the throat of the flower
7. Using a very fine paintbrush and pale green liquid colouring, mark 3 short fine lines from the centre of the flower extending almost to half way up each of the 5 petals.

Buds

Make a small semi-tapered ball of paste and attach these to separate pieces of wire. Vary the size of the buds slightly.

Leaves

Alternate in pairs along the wire. A small ball of green forms a junction between the two top leaves.

Calyx

Paint a small green calyx at the base of each flower and bud.

Honeysuckle

1. Cut a short length of wire and tape 6 stamens to it, leaving one long stigma. Curve the stamens over the finger or draw the blade of the scissors across them to curve.
2. Hollow-cone a piece of white modelling paste and divide the rim into 5 equal portions. Slash 2 adjacent cuts fairly long for the centre top petal and mitre to a thin top point widening to the base of the cut.

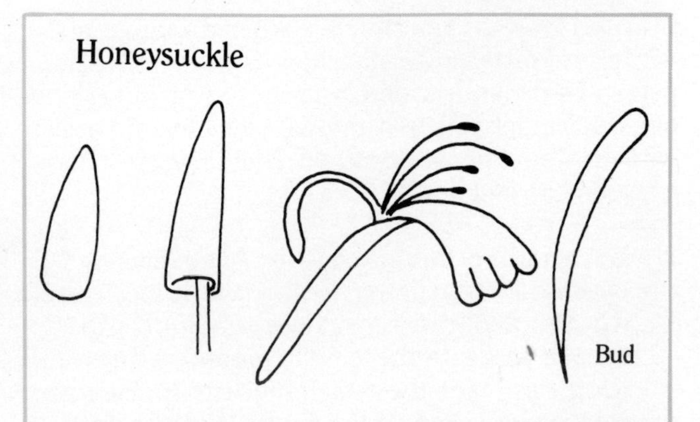

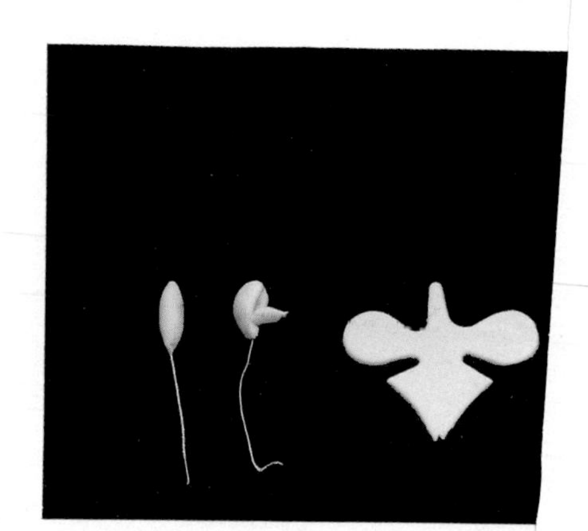

the paste and cutting cleanly a
sharp scalpel.

2. Using a ball tool, curve the w
of the throat.

Sepals

1. Roll out the paste and cut th
lightly on veiner, or dried c
2. Fold and pinch a centre rid
the sepal, or lay the sepal alo
pinch the ridge on the top

Lower base sepals

Repeat the previous directions
pinched ridge is the back of the
side as for the centre petal.

Top side sepals

Roll, cut vein and ridge as previ
is on the top side of each sepal a
as a pair.

To assemble

1. Place a piece of foil across
or similar vessel.
2. Make a centre hole in t
sepals, centre and lowe
triangle.
3. Attach each with water,
page 112).
4. Now position the top si
previous 3. Attach with
5. Place the labellum (or t
tion and insert the w
centre. Dampen with w
dry completely before re
glass and foil.

3. The remaining cuts are more shallow and rounded softly.
4. Turn the top centre long petal back into a gentle curve; turn the 4 small petals on the lower edge to a soft curve and insert the wire. Allow to dry.
5. Dust some flowers pale cream; leave some white.

Buds

These are elongated, thicker at the top, tapered at the base.

Jasmine

This beautiful climber comes in shades of pink, yellow and white, pink and the white being the most common.

1. Shape a long hollow cone from a piece of white modelling paste, cut the top edge into 5 equal sections. Cut a semi-rounded point to each petal.
2. Smooth the edges by holding the petal between the thumb and index fingers and turn it back away from the centre of the flower.
3. Dampen a piece of fine wire, knotted, insert it through the cone and secure it to the base of the paste.
4. Into the centre of each flower, pipe a small green royal icing stamen (or insert a manufactured stamen). Allow the flower to dry before dusting with chalk. It is necessary to dust only the back of the flowers. The pink chalk used here had a tinge of lilac powder added to it.

Buds

Place a long and tapered piece of modelling paste over a fine wire. Shape a bulged cone to the top.

Honeysuckle

Jasmine

Full blown rose

Full blown rose

1. Secure a cluster of stamens to a fine wire and tint them with egg yellow colour mixed with a touch of caramel brown.
2. Use the small, medium and large rose cutter and cut 5 or 6 petals of each size from the modelling paste for each row. Smooth the cut edge with your fingertips and softly flute with an anger tool. Place the petal onto a small square of aluminium foil. Press into the centre of the petal with the cushion of the thumb; at the same time turn the top of the petal backwards with the other hand, allowing the foil to support the petal until dry. Repeat this method with all the petals.
3. When dry tint to the desired shade.

To assemble

1. Pipe a large dot of royal icing onto a piece of waxed paper. Attach the outside petals in a spiral fashion, slightly overlapping each other.
2. Use a little more royal icing for each row to attach the petals into the space left where the two outside petals overlap.
3. Position the small centre petals, leaving space to insert the cluster of stamens. There should be no royal icing visible where petals are attached.

Note: Use your own judgment as to how many centre petals the rose will take — there is no need to overcrowd.

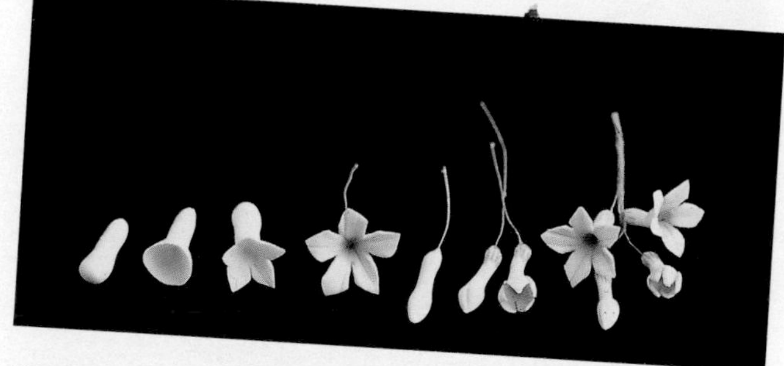

Stephanotis

Stephanotis

1. Using a white piece of modelling paste about the size of a large pea, hollow-cone it to a long trumpet then cut the top edge into 5 equal sections to form the petals.
2. With a pair of sharp scissors, cut each petal to a semi-rounded point. Take each individual petal between the thumb and index fingers to smooth, then turn it back slightly from the centre of the flower.
3. Insert a piece of finely-knotted wire and attach it firmly to the paste. The flower has a slightly waisted shape from under the petals, which rounds off again at the base of the flower. Allow to dry.
4. Using a pale green chalk dust the inside of the cone lightly; also the base of the flower where it joins the calyx.
5. Hollow-cone a tiny piece of green paste and cut it into a 5-pointed calyx. Dampen the centre and insert the Stephanotis while the calyx is still soft.

Buds

1. A small pea-sized piece of paste is shaped to a long tapered cone over a piece of fine wire which has been dampened. Round the top of the bud then shape it into a soft cone-like tip. Mark the unopened petals with a small knife.
2. Dust the top and the base of the bud lightly with pale green chalk. Allow to dry before attaching it to the calyx.

Full blown roses give impact to this beautiful cake decorated by Lyn Coltman.

Cattleya orchid

Column

1. Take a small cone-shaped piec paste.
2. Insert a short length of wire fr With a small ball tool, groove the underside of the column.
3. Pinch a ∨ with a pair of twe and to the centre of the colu egg-yellow and allow to dry

Labellum (or throat)

1. Roll the paste out, cut by pl and cutting cleanly with a sh a specific orchid cutter for
2. Vein over a dried corn husk edge deeply. Dampen the b attach it in a cone-like fashi to dry over a ball of cotton

Sepals (unfluted)

1. Cut out 3 sepals by inser into a log-shaped piece of right of the wire until the the petal. Cut the petal a and allow to dry into a cotton wool. Repeat twic

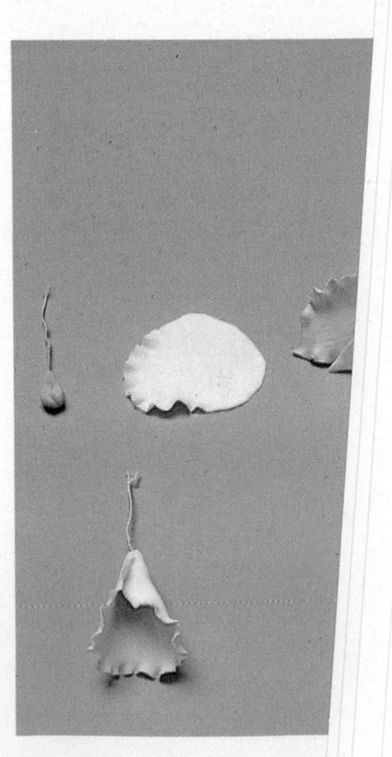

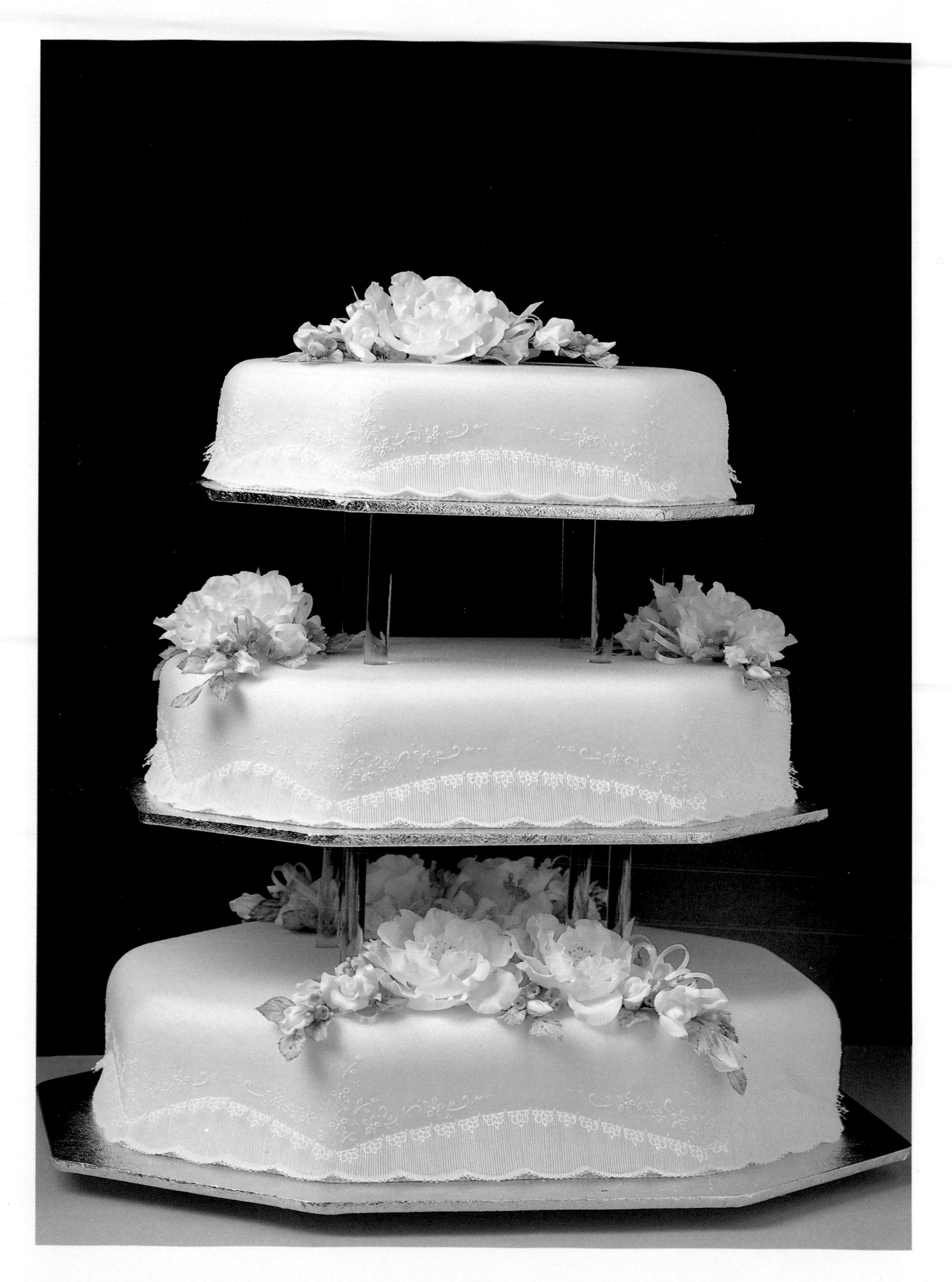

8. Allow the flower to dry completely before colouring. If possible colour from a real flower using liquid food colouring. When dry, paint the fine black vein lines onto petals 3, 4 and 5.

Buds

Hook and dampen the wire, hollow-cone a piece of paste and cut it into 5 rounded petals. Flute each petal slightly. Insert the wire and fold the petals in towards the centre. Allow to dry before inserting this bud into a calyx.

Leaf

See diagram.

Note: The instructions for the pansy are identical. The only difference is in placing the top right hand petal into position first and overlapping it with the left hand petal.

Wild violet

1. Take a pea-sized piece of white modelling paste and hollow-cone it out.
2. Cut it as diagrams illustrate.
   Cuts 1 and 2 will form the widest petal at the base of the flower.
   Cut 3 bisects the remaining position.
   Cuts 4 and 5 bisect, to make 4 equal portions for the smaller petals. The violet has 5 petals including the large one at the base.
3. With a pair of sharp-pointed small scissors, round the edges of the large petal and cut the 4 smaller petals into a semi point.
4. Press a small ball tool into the larger petal to cup it slightly. Smooth the two side petals by pressing lightly between the thumb and index finger, before turning each back a little from the centre of the flower.

Wild violet

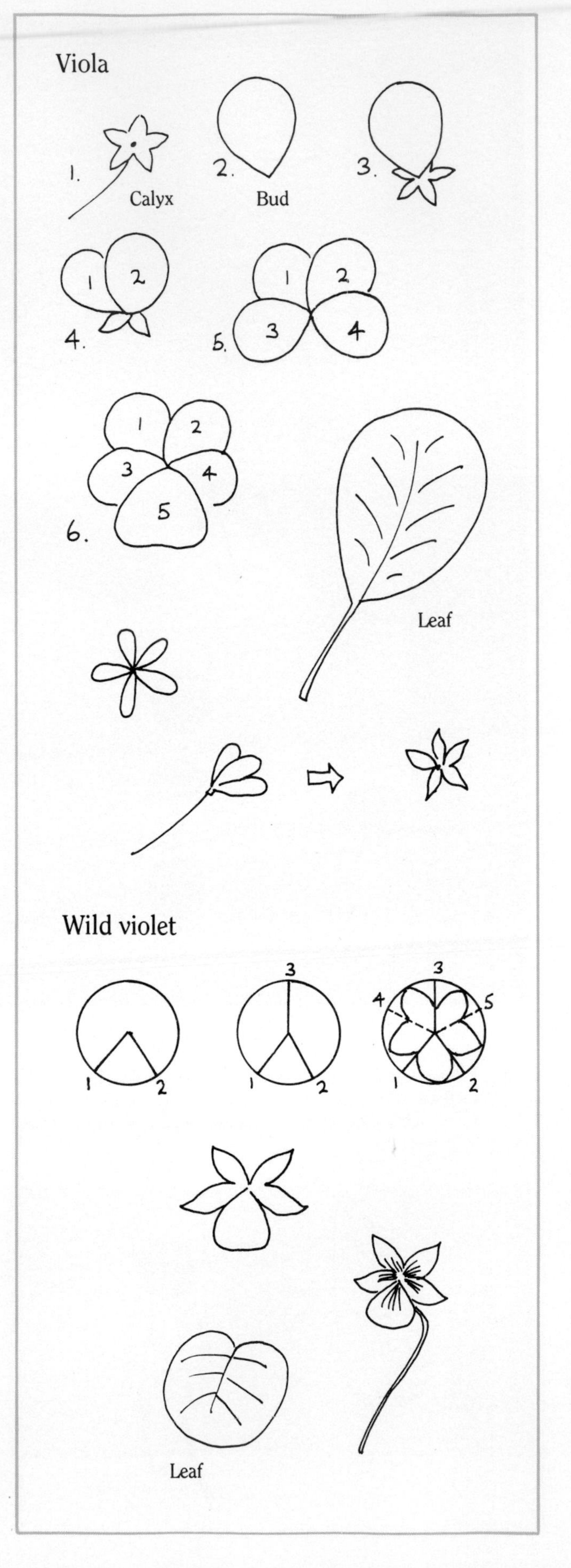

5. Repeat this method for the two top petals, stretching the paste a little to lengthen. Allow to dry.
6. With liquid food colouring, paint the centre of the throat with a shading of buttercup yellow.
7. Mix violet and blue liquid colour, dilute with water and test the colour on a piece of white paste or paper until the desired shade is obtained. Paint with irregular strokes from the centre of the petal outwards, merging the colour into white approximately two-thirds up each petal. This will leave a white margin around the outer edges of the flower.
8. When dry, pipe a pale green stamen in the centre of each flower.

Leaves

Cut according to pattern, vein and indent slightly with a large ball tool to give a slight curve.

Driftwood arrangement of Viola and Honeysuckle made by Mary Lynas.

Waratah

1. Colour the modelling paste a basic red.
2. Mould approximately 15 small carrot-shaped pieces to form the crown of the flower.
3. Make approximately 20 comma-shaped pieces and curve these over the finger slightly.
   Each successive row will require 20-25 commas, slightly longer than the preceding row. (There are approximately 5 rows.) The sizes will range from ½ cm to 3 cm lengths, prior to curving. These may vary proportionately according to the size of the flower.
4. Allow all pieces to thoroughly dry before shaping the dome.

Waratah

Dome

1. Take a walnut-sized piece of paste and mould it into a dome. Using a probe or the point of a knitting needle, make a small hole into the centre top of the dome. Dampen the hole and insert a carrot-shaped piece into it, work around this in rows using the carrot-sized pieces to form the crown of the flower.
2. Continue to probe holes to insert the rows of comma pieces, graduating the sizes until the dome is completely covered. Each hole should be dampened before the comma is inserted. Allow to firm before attaching the three rows of bracts.

Bracts

1. The first row consists of 5 small bracts, shaped, veined and attached to the base of the dome with a little water.
2. The second and third rows consist of 7-9 larger bracts attached in the same way.

Note: Domes may also be made by piping a series of small to large teardrops with royal icing over the modelling paste base to form the centre crown. Working on a row for row basis, increase the pressure to form rows of graduated teardrops, until completely covered from top to base.

To colour

When the waratah is completely dry, paint it all over with liquid red food colouring or dust it with red chalk.

Leaves

Leaves are broad and serrated and look rather heavy. If there is other foliage in the spray I omit these leaves.

FOLIAGE

Nature offers a vast assortment of leaves. Often the decorator uses the basic green colours to accompany floral arrangements of sugar art, whereas the beautiful autumn toning of leaves such as the Maple, Oak, and Nandina could provide an alternative complementary background to the work.

Privet and variegated ivy leaves contrasted with yellow borders and splashes of yellow throughout the green are visually appealing and should be used to accompany suitable arrangements.

Ferns

Ferns such as maidenhair, have a more natural appearance if stems from the living plant are picked and allowed to dry flat between the pages of a book before being used in conjunction with royal icing or flower paste.

1. Cut the dried leaf of the maidenhair back almost to the stem, leaving a small triangular piece on which to work.
2. Place the prepared fern on a piece of waxed paper and pipe dots of green royal icing over each piece.
3. When finished, completely cover the fern with a top layer of waxed paper, waxed side on the royal icing. With a wooden skewer or small rolling pin, lightly roll across the paper and flatten the royal icing dots.
4. *Do not* remove the fern from between the waxed paper layers until it is completely dry.

Small fern cutters are available; these are suitable for modelling paste cut-outs which are attached to the tip of each stem with a little gum arabic solution. Cover the fern with waxed paper. Roll *lightly* across the top. Allow to dry thoroughly before removing the paper.

Note: Choose the strongest natural stems for this method of decorating.

Maiden hair fern

Maiden hair fern

Spaghetti fern

This is completely edible. Original idea from Mrs J N Clack of South Africa.

1. Boil the spaghetti in water with green food colouring until tender. Drain and place the pasta in different-shaped strands to dry on a flat board covered with plastic clingwrap.
2. When completely dry, break the shapes into the desired lengths and glue them together with gum arabic solution.
3. Paint generously with gum arabic to strengthen. Allow this to dry. This may require a few applications before removing the fern from the board.

Ribbon grass

1. Take a piece of creamy white modelling paste. Roll it out thinly and cut a blade leaf from it.
2. To shape, drape the grass blade over a suitable curve to dry, e.g. a jar or a tin.
3. Paint a green stripe along each side of the leaf, leaving the centre strip its natural creamy colour.

Foliage (clockwise from bottom left) Sweetpea, Gypsophila, Maple, Nandina and Rose leaf.

Wheat

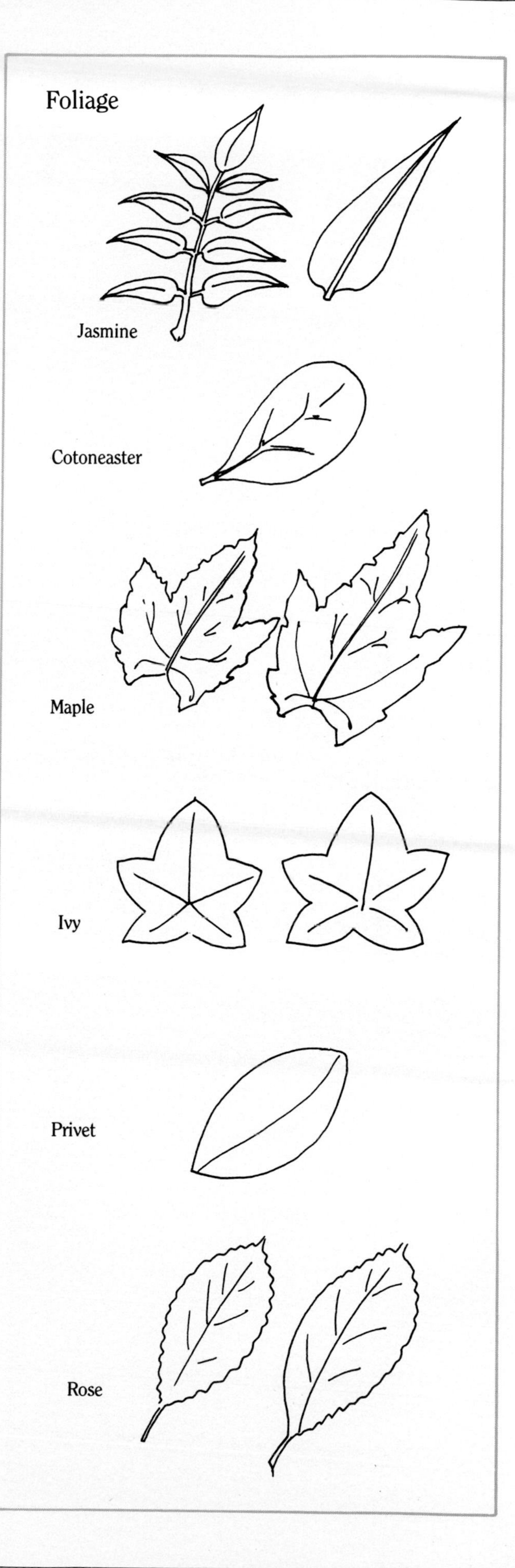

Moulded wheat

1. Colour a small amount of modelling paste into a deep creamy yellow. Remove the tips from both ends of the stamens, leaving only the cotton thread.
2. Take a small piece of sugar paste about the size of a cooked grain of rice, or a little larger. Taper it to one end and insert the dampened cotton through the paste. Allow the cotton to protrude from the top and the bottom of the wheat. Pinch the centre of the paste with tweezers to flatten.
3. Approximately 30 wheat grains will be required for each stalk.
4. When dry these may be attached to a medium wire or cocktail stick with florist tape.
5. When assembled, dust over with powdered chalk to improve the colour of the wheat and to colour the white cotton of the stamens.

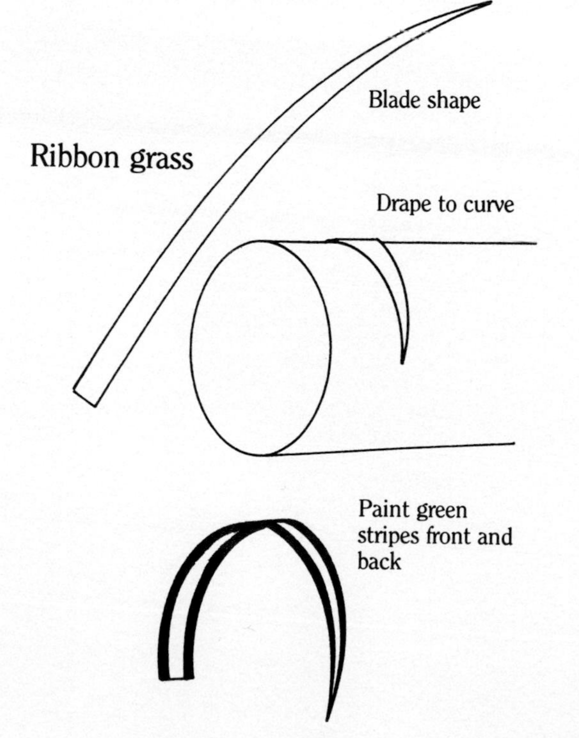

SUGAR ART

Baby and ballerina shoes

The same technique is suitable for both.

Baby's shoes

1. Take 2 equal-sized pieces of sugar paste and mould them into log-shaped pieces. Cover one with a tumbler while working on the other to prevent it drying.
2. Place a ball tool (or index finger) in the centre of the paste, indent the ball tool and work the paste around it to form the toe.
3. Continue to hollow and shape the inside of the shoe and also around the ankle and back of the foot by working the top until it has thinned sufficiently to form a neat edge.
4. Work with the fingers to shape under the sole to gain a softly moulded edge, rather than a flat angular finish.

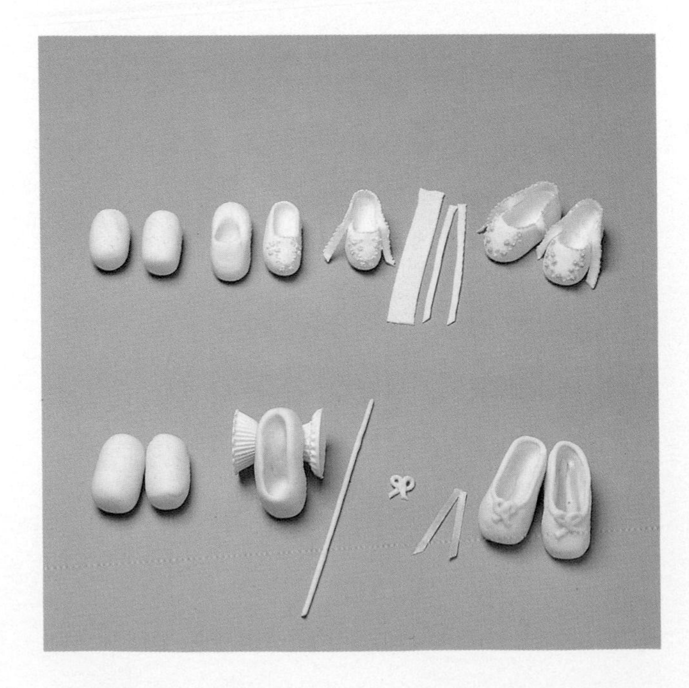

5. Repeat the instructions for the second shoe to this point. Make sure both shoes are the same size when finished.
6. Pipe an embroidery pattern of small forget-me-nots, or the design of your choice over the toe.
7. Roll a thin strip of paste and cut the ankle straps approximately 3 mm wide. Cover one to prevent it drying while attaching the other.
8. Use royal icing the same colour as the shoes to attach the ankle strap or a gum arabic glue solution.
9. Trim the strap to the length required and neaten across the top of the strap and front of the shoe with a very small "teardrop".

Ballerina shoes

1. Use the same method as the baby's shoes. When the shoe has been shaped, give a curve to the sole and set to dry over a suitable curve which will elevate the sole and the heel, yet allow the toe to remain flat on the table or board.
2. Shoes must be identical in size. Take a small piece of paste and roll it into a thin roulex, sufficiently long to go completely around the top of the shoe. Attach this with gum arabic solution.
3. Make a tiny bow from the leftover pieces of roulex, attach these to the front of each shoe.
4. Using a 3 mm satin ribbon cut 2 lengths for each shoe for ties and attach.

Dance, Ballerina, Dance *See page 51 for Tulle appliqué leaves and embroidery.*

Bibs with the flounce

1. Roll out the fondant (or modelling paste) to a medium fine thickness.
2. Using the pattern on page 125, cut neatly around the edge with a sharp scalpel.
3. With a tapered anger tool or knitting needle, press into the fondant and roll to produce a soft flounce. Work quickly around the lower edge while doing this, before the fondant or paste dries.
4. Pipe an embroidery pattern suitable for the occasion.
5. Flood or paint a motif as the central feature on the bib.
6. Neaten the neck edge with a fine teardrop, then pipe a row of tiny scallops below this line. Finish the back neck with a piped button and loop.

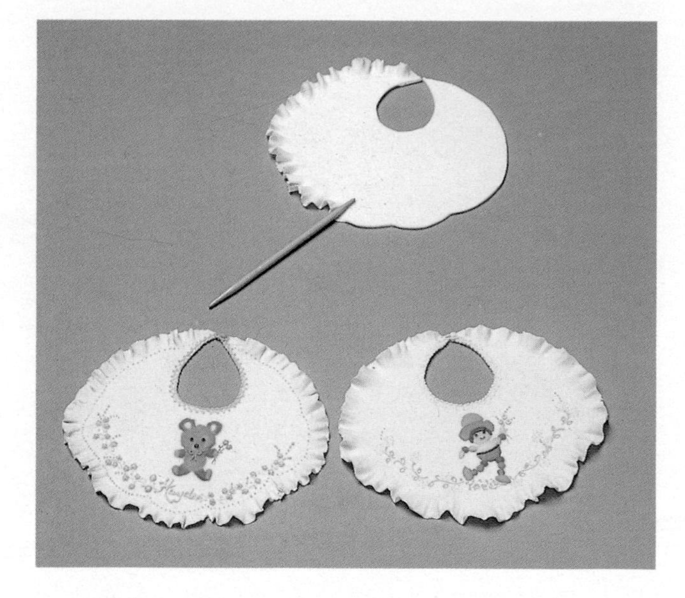

Candlestick

1. Roll the modelling paste out thinly and cut an 8 cm circle with a pastry cutter.
2. Press this round of paste into a muffin tin or patty pan until it takes its shape. Then remove it from the tin and allow to dry thoroughly.
3. Take a log-shaped piece of paste approximately 2.5 cm in length and cup it out at the top with the handle of a paintbrush or suitable tool. Turn back a small lip edge and allow to dry.

Candle

1. Roll out a log-shaped piece of paste, the thickness of the candle required and approximately 7 cm in length.

Note: The diameter of the candle will be determined by the size of the hole made in the candlestick to hold it.

2. Make a groove in the top of the candle and pierce a hole in the centre for the wick.

Handle

1. Roll out the paste, cut a strip to the width and length required (approximately 1 cm wide). Shape and allow to dry.
2. Assemble the pieces by attaching them with royal icing. Allow to dry before neatening the edges with pipe work.

Wax

Pipe royal icing from below the wick to run down the side of the candle.

Flower fairies

Dress these little figures up to represent flowers such as daisies, buttercups, bluebells, roses etc. It is time-consuming but fun.

Head

1. Moulds suitable for the face and head are available in some cake decorating supply stores. These enable the decorator to form the head by pushing a piece of flesh-coloured paste into the mould, then removing and shaping any excess paste to the back of the head before inserting a short length of spaghetti up through the neck and into the head for support.
2. If moulds are not available, shape a small piece of paste into a ball, mark in the eyes and mouth and attach a tiny piece of paste for the nose.

3. Insert a small length of spaghetti through the tapered neck and up into the head. When dry paint in the features and pipe the hair.

Arms

1. Form a small piece of flesh-coloured paste into a sausage. Cut it into 2 equal lengths. Cover one length while working on the other to prevent it from drying.
2. Proportion the arm and taper in at the wrist and the elbow. Flatten the hand and cut a V for the thumb then three cuts to form each finger.
3. Roll the fingers lightly to shape and press a small ball tool into the palm to give a natural curve to the hand.
4. Bend the arm at the elbow as required and allow it to dry flat on a piece of sponge foam.
5. Repeat this method for the other arm.

Legs

1. Form the flesh-coloured paste into a sausage and cut it into 2, proportionate in size to the body. Cover one piece while working on the other. Taper in at the ankle and the knee. Bend and shape the foot.
2. Insert a length of spaghetti through the leg to extend below the foot and above the top leg for approximately 2 cm.
3. Shape the leg and allow it to dry on a piece of sponge foam.
4. Repeat this method for the other leg.

Body

1. Form a piece of flesh-coloured paste into a sausage. Shape to narrow it at the waist, and flatten it slightly.
2. Make an indentation with a ball tool where the legs will fit into the body and where the arms will fit into the shoulders. Brush gum arabic solution into these holes before inserting the legs and arms into the soft paste. Allow the body to set before dressing the fairy. Bodies may also be formed as a pear shape and the legs cut and shaped at the same time.

Torso tunic

1. Torso tunic for the pear-shaped body is formed as a Mexican hat, hollowed out and cut into petals or cut with a flower cutter.
2. Collar may be cut with a calyx cutter.
3. If the figure is to be in a sitting position, drape the body over a small box and place the legs into position.

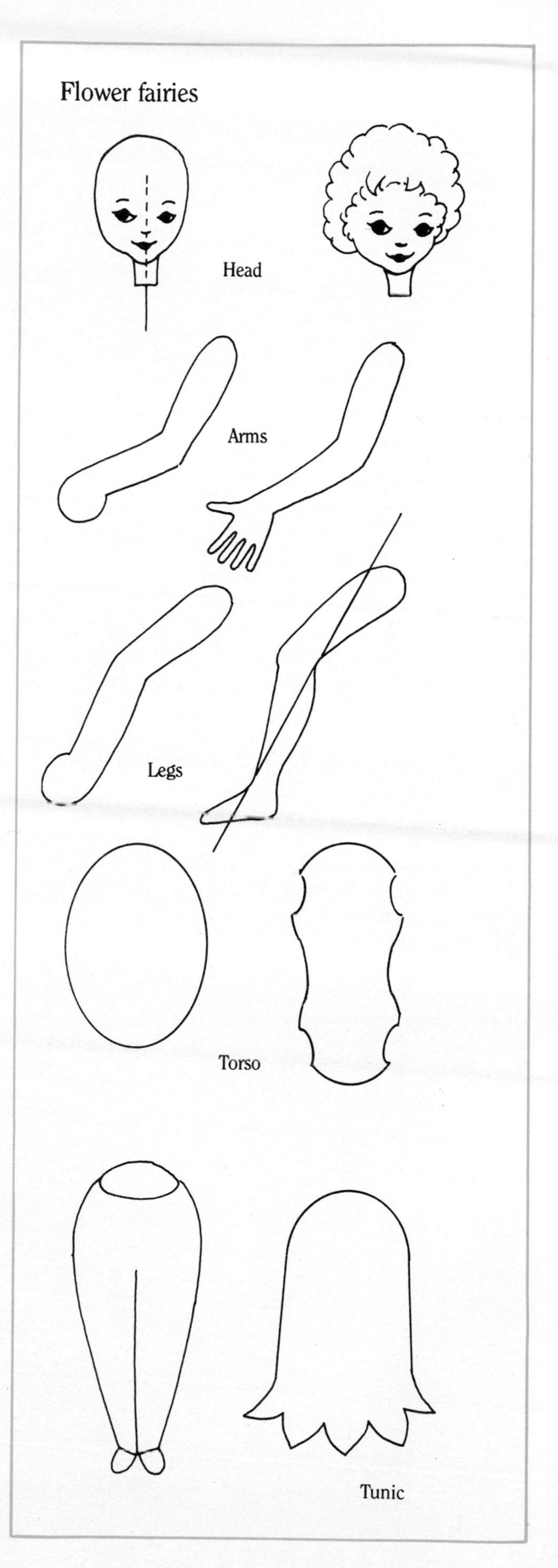

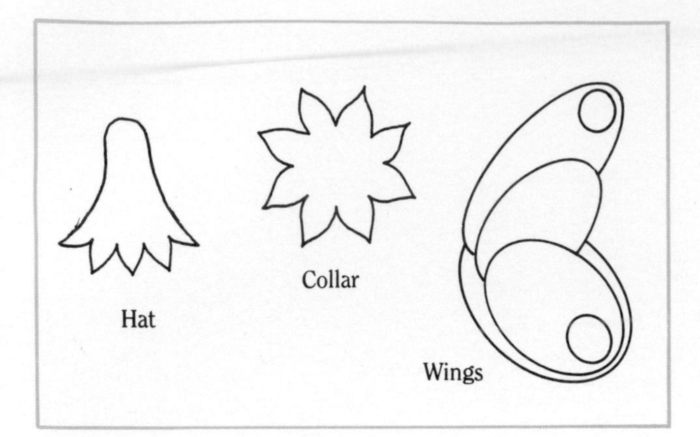

Fairy wings

Roll modelling paste very thinly and cut the pattern. Shape wings slightly over a ball of cottonwool and allow to dry before painting in the colours. These are attached with royal icing to the body and supported until dry.

Jelly bean clowns

These funny little characters are suitable for children's party cakes. They may also be used as name place settings for the young guests.

1. Colour a small quantity of flesh-coloured fondant.
2. Roll a piece into a ball about the size of a marble.
3. Make a small hole in the face for the nose and roll a tiny piece of red fondant into the shape of a carrot. Dampen and insert the point into the hole and round the top into a ball for the nose.
4. Place the head on a cocktail stick and paint the face. Pipe the hair and top it off with a piped or moulded hat. Allow to dry.
5. Cut a small round of waxed paper and pipe the feet (shoes) onto it with No. 8 shell tube.
6. The shoes are piped as 2 separate shells close together. If a round toe is preferred, the top of the shell is used as the front. If a pointed toe is desired, reverse the position, so that the pointed ends are to the front. Allow to firm.
7. Large-sized jelly beans are required for the body. Insert a cocktail stick into the base of the jelly bean for ease when handling.
8. Pipe the buttons or pompoms down the centre front with No. 8 shell tube.
9. Pipe the arms with the same tube from each shoulder. Pipe gloved hands using No. 1 tube.
10. Using a No. 20 petal tube, pipe a frill across the top of the arms and around the neck area.
11. Remove the cocktail stick from under the head and attach the head into the wet frill and allow to dry.
12. Pipe a frill using the same No. 20 tube over the top of the shoes.
13. Remove the cocktail stick from the jelly bean and place the clown into position, over the shoes and into the wet frill.
14. The clown may require a little support until set; particularly if the royal icing has been too soft.

Note: To produce multi-coloured royal icing, stripe the inside of the bag with a paintbrush and paste colours before filling with royal icing.

Jelly bean clowns, a joy for any child's party.

Fantasy in the Garden *These flower fairies will delight the young.*

ADVICE TO THE EXHIBITOR

As an international and national judge of many years standing, I feel the following advice may be helpful to exhibitors as well as new judges.

1. When entering any competition, it is vitally important for the exhibitor and the judge to study the schedule and the conditions of entry carefully. They must know and understand what is allowed and disallowed and abide by these specific rules at all times.
2. Entry forms should be tendered early and the closing time and date for delivery of the exhibits should be kept well in mind to avoid last minute "rushes" and/or unexpected eventualities. "Rushed" work so often results in loss of finesse.
3. Quality not quantity is important.
4. A perfect or near to perfect cake cover is essential. It is pointless to be able to execute beautiful pipe work and moulded work, yet poorly cover a cake. Should the cover not be up to standard re-cover the cake, instead of trying to camouflage the faults in the next phases of the work.
5. In tiered cakes, grade the work, e.g. when using piped embroidery and lace, according to the design each tier is identical but reduced proportionately in size.
6. Creativity and the ability of the decorator to introduce new ideas should never be overlooked by any judge; creativity is the life blood of our wonderful world of sugar and the decorator should receive recognition by the judge for presenting new and innovative ideas and techniques.
7. Remember the judge looks to the back of the work as well as the front. Flowers should show calyx, buds and leaves and be as close to nature as possible. Near enough is not good enough. If possible, model the flower from a natural one from the garden. Should this not be possible, refer to some of the excellent books on flowers, available from libraries and shops.
8. Decorate with health and safety in mind. It is important not to use materials that may be injurious to health — such as synthetic nylon used in place of cotton stamens, or craft glues used to attach sugar pieces. Children's cakes should be completely edible.
9. Visual impact is important; try not to over decorate. It is a wise person who knows when to stop.
10. Pre-plan the design and know your goals before you start.
11. The cake must be suitable to the class in which it is entered and easily identified as such.
12. The judge is governed by the same rules of the competition as the exhibitor. It is as disappointing for the judge to rule an exhibit out as N.A.S. (not as schedule) as it is for the exhibitor who has entered work not acceptable in its class.
13. Great care should be taken in the preparation and covering of all base boards. Cleats or runners should be attached for ease in lifting and moving the exhibits. These base runners should be covered in the same covering as the boards, or painted to tone with the exhibit.
14. Boards used to support tiered cakes should be neatly covered top and bottom.
15. Royal icing should be the correct consistency e.g. shell work should be firm enough to hold its shape whereas royal icing used for embroidery, lace and extension or floating bridgework should be soft enough to flow well from the tube yet hold and maintain clearly its well-defined form.
16. Enter competitive work prepared to accept the judge's decision as final.

This beautiful arrangement, so close to nature, is moulded from modelling paste and presented in a hand moulded vase.

RECIPES

Apricot jam purée

Apricot jam purée is a glaze used for brushing the surface of the cake prior to covering it with almond or marzipan paste and plastic icing.

1. Rub 3 or 4 tablespoons of the jam through a sieve. Add sufficient water to reduce it to a thick syrup of brushing consistency.
2. Bring the mixture to the boil, then allow it to cool slightly before applying with a pastry brush to the cake.
3. By brushing the jam puree over the cake while it is still warm, the decorator is able to get a *thin*, sticky, coating, whereas cold jam is inclined to brush on too thick.

Note: Boiling the jam helps prevent fermentation.

Almond paste

1.5 kg pure icing sugar, sifted
500 g ground almonds
5 egg yolks
3 tablespoons lemon juice
3 tablespoons brandy or sweet sherry
almond essence (optional, to taste)

1. Mix the dry ingredients thoroughly.
2. Beat the eggs, juice and brandy together.
3. Make a well in the centre and add the liquid gradually until the paste is firm enough to roll.

Note: If the mixture is too soft, add some extra sifted icing sugar. If too dry add extra fruit juice or alcohol.

4. Place the paste in an airtight container or plastic bag until ready to use.

The almond base cover should be applied about 2 days prior to covering the cake with fondant or plastic icing. This will allow the oil in the almonds to dry. Should this amount of time not be possible, dissolve a little gelatine in water and brush it all over the almond paste cover. This will prevent the oil from the almonds seeping through and staining the fondant.

If using marzipan meal as a substitute for the ground almonds, allow the cake to stand at least 12 hours before applying the fondant cover over the marzipan paste surface.

Plastic icing

This well-tested recipe is economical, reliable and easy to use and will cover a 20 × 20 cm cake.

1 kg pure icing sugar
120 ml liquid glucose
15 g gelatine (3 level teaspoons)
23 ml glycerine
60 ml water
lemon or almond essence to taste

1. Sieve icing sugar into a large bowl.
2. Disperse gelatine in water in a small saucepan.
3. Place the saucepan over a gentle heat until gelatine has dissolved (do not allow to boil).
4. Remove from the heat, add glucose and glycerine, stir to combine.
5. Add the liquid to the icing sugar gradually, mixing well with the hands until combined into a firm dough-like paste.
6. Add flavouring to suit personal taste.
7. Transfer the mixture to a board lightly dusted with cornflour and knead well until the mixture is smooth, pliable and elastic. It should resemble a plasticine consistency.
8. The icing is now ready for immediate use, or it may be stored in an airtight container until required.

Note: Should the mixture be too soft, work some extra icing sugar into it. If too firm a little hot water will soften it to the correct consistency.

I Love a Bedtime Story *Who could resist this adorable bear attired for bed. Bear tins are available from some decorating supply stores, or the cake may be cut and sculptured to shape by the decorator. Instructions for the candlestick are on page 102.*

Bedtime
Stories
H. C. ANDERSON.

Reliable recipes for fruit cakes

It is most important to use a well-tested and reliable recipe when baking a rich fruit cake which is usually the basis for most Australian special occasion cakes.

The decorator will spend many hours preparing and decorating this cake, so it should be as good to eat as it is to look at.

The following recipe will yield a two-tier wedding cake using 25 × 25 cm and 15 × 15 cm cake tins.

Wash, dry and prepare all fruit, remove any small stalks or seeds before cutting the larger pieces to the required size.

Before starting to mix the cake, weigh and measure all the ingredients and place them on a tray ready for use.

Rich fruit cake I

625 g butter
625 g sugar
3 teaspoons Parisian essence
15 medium eggs
650 g sultanas
650 g raisins cut in 4
600 g currants
375 g mixed peel, chopped
185 g blanched almonds, chopped
125 g dates, chopped
125 g prunes, chopped
125 g glacé ginger, chopped
125 g glacé cherries, cut in 4
1½ teaspoons cinnamon
1½ teaspoons mixed spice
½ teaspoon nutmeg
780 g plain flour (sifted)
300 ml brandy

1. Preheat the oven to 150°C (300°F).
2. Line the baking tins (see page 60).
3. Cream the butter and sugar, add the Parisian essence.
4. Add beaten eggs one at a time and continue beating.
5. Add the prepared fruit, nuts and all the dry ingredients.
6. Add the brandy and mix well.
7. Place the mixture into the prepared tins and bake at 150°C (300°F) for the first 30 minutes.
8. Decrease the oven heat to 130°C (275°F) for the remainder of the cooking time. The large cake will take approximately 5 hours. The small one will take approximately 3 hours.

Note: If the top of the cake is browning too quickly, cover it with a piece of greaseproof or brown paper half way through the cooking time. Remove the paper 15 minutes before the cake is ready and allow the cake to finish baking before removing it from the oven.

While still warm, wrap the tin and cake in a large towel and allow to cool. Cakes for special occasions should be baked about 6 weeks prior to the event. This allows the flavour to mature and ensures that the cake will cut cleanly without crumbling.

Rich fruit cake II

250 g butter
250 g brown sugar
5 large eggs
1 teaspoon mixed spice
1 teaspoon mace
1 teaspoon cinnamon
1 teaspoon ground ginger
2 teaspoons lemon zest
2 teaspoons Parisian essence
2 teaspoons glycerine
1 tablespoon marmalade
1 tablespoon lemon juice
300 g plain flour
1 teaspoon salt
250 g sultanas
250 g currants
250 g raisins
125 g mixed peel
125 g glace cherries
125 g blanched almonds
60 g glace ginger
60 g figs (or prunes)
60 g dates
60 g glace apricots
½ cup brandy

Prepare the fruit, cut raisins into 3, sultanas into 2, cherries into half. Chop the figs, dates and glace fruits. Chop the nuts and keep separately.

Mix all fruit together in a bowl and pour the brandy over the fruit. Allow to stand 24 hours.

1. Preheat oven to 150°C (300°F).
2. Paper line a 20 × 20 cm tin or a 23 cm round tin (see page 60).
3. Cream the butter and sugar.
4. Add the eggs one at a time, beating well after each addition.
5. Add the spices, marmalade, zest, glycerine, lemon juice and Parisian essence.
6. Add the prepared fruit, alternately with the sifted flour and salt. Add the nuts and mix well.
7. Place the mixture into the prepared tin. Drop or bang the tin onto the bench to settle any air pockets before placing it into the oven.

Someone's Halo is Slipping *Bas relief angels suitable for Holy Communion or a Christmas cake. A template for the angels is on page 120.*

8. Bake in a moderately slow oven 150°F (300°F) for 1 hour before reducing the heat to 130°C (250°F) for the remainder of the cooking time. The cake will take approximately 3½ hours to bake. Test with a metal skewer.

Note: To prevent the cake browning too much during the cooking period, cover the top with a piece of grease-proof or brown paper half way through the baking time. Remove the paper 15 minutes prior to the cake being removed from the oven.

Allow the cake to cool in the tin, cover with a towel while still warm.

Gum arabic (glue solution)

This edible solution is excellent for attaching sugar paste petals and leaves.

1 teaspoon gum arabic
2 teaspoons water

Heat together these two ingredients, then strain the liquid into a small lidded container. Keep refrigerated when not in use.

Gelatine glaze

30 ml water
2 teaspoons gelatine
1 teaspoon liquid glucose

1. Place the water into a small bowl or cup and sprinkle the gelatine over it. Place the container into the microwave oven for approximately 14 seconds on medium high, until the gelatine dissolves. *Do not allow the mixture to boil.*
2. Remove the bowl from the microwave, add the liquid glucose and stir well to combine.
3. This glaze should be applied to the sugar piece with a brush while still hot to impart a high gloss.
4. When not in use, store the mixture in an airtight container in the refrigerator. Reheat before using again.

The mixture may be made in a small saucepan on top of the stove, if a microwave is not available.

Pastillage

⅔ cup granulated sugar
240 ml water (or sufficient to just cover the sugar)
1 slightly rounded tablespoon gelatine
1 kg pure icing sugar, sifted

1. Place the granulated sugar in a small saucepan and cover it with water. Heat gently until the sugar dissolves, stirring occasionally in the early stages of heating.
2. Boil without stirring until the syrup reaches the thread stage, test by taking a little syrup in a spoon, allow it to cool and press it between thumb and forefinger for the thread.
3. Allow the syrup to cool slightly before pouring it onto the gelatine and stir until the gelatine has dissolved, or the gelatine may be added to the sugar syrup to dissolve.
4. Add half the sifted icing sugar in small quantities and beat it in with a wooden spoon, as if mixing royal icing.
5. When the mixture resembles whipped cream, cover, seal and allow to cool.
6. Add the remaining sifted icing sugar and work it in until the dough is firm enough to roll without sticking.
7. The secret of pastillage is to allow it to cool and to work it dry not soft.
8. This mixture is ideal for structural designs such as churches or buildings because of its firmness and drying ability. However, all pattern pieces must be turned and reversed several times to dry thoroughly. Store pastillage airtight.

Sticky gum sugar paste

1 tablespoon fondant or modelling paste
2 teaspoons water

1. Heat and mix the above ingredients until a syrup-like mixture results.
2. This edible glue is ideal for attaching petals and leaves when moulding. It forms an invisible join when the same colour paste is used as that of the flower or leaf.
3. Should the mixture appear too thick, add a little more hot water until the right consistency is obtained.
4. Store in an airtight container.

Bernice's modelling paste (or flower paste)

3 level teaspoons gelatine
60 ml water
10 ml liquid glucose, measured in a medicine glass
500 g pure icing sugar

1. Place gelatine and water in a small saucepan. Allow mixture to disperse.
2. Place the saucepan over gentle heat until the gelatine has dissolved. *Do not stir and do not boil.*
3. Remove from the heat, add the glucose and stir to dissolve it into the liquid.
4. Allow the mixture to cool slightly before adding it gradually to the icing sugar in a bowl. Knead well until all the icing sugar has been absorbed and forms a firm paste.
5. Remove the mixture from the bowl and knead it well on a board, lightly dusted with cornflour. Continue to knead until the paste is smooth, elastic and pliable, resembling a plasticine consistency.
6. Do not allow the paste to remain exposed to the air. After mixing, place the contents into a sealed airtight container.
7. Colour and use as desired.
8. If this mixture appears too soft add a little extra sifted icing sugar. If too dry, add drops of hot water. This is a quick drying paste which, once moulded, will retain its shape under wet and humid conditions.

Modelling paste (slow drying)

2 cups pure icing sugar, sifted
1 small egg white
3 teaspoons gum tragacanth
2 teaspoons gelatine
4 teaspoons water

1. Grease a bowl with white vegetable shortening and add 1 cup sifted icing sugar. Sprinkle the gum tragacanth over the sugar and place the bowl in a microwave oven for approximately 14 seconds on medium-high until the contents are warm (not hot).
2. Disperse the gelatine in water and dissolve it in the microwave. *Do not allow the mixture to boil.* Heat for approximately 10-14 seconds.
3. Add to the warmed sugar mixture in the bowl. Mix well, then add the egg white, and the remaining cup of icing sugar.
4. Transfer the paste to a greased clean bowl or greased bench top and knead well. It will be necessary to smear the hands occasionally with the vegetable shortening.
5. Continue to knead until the mixture is well combined and pliable, then place it in a plastic bag and sealed container. Allow the paste to stand at least 12 hours in the refrigerator before using.

Note: If a microwave is not available, place the basin over a bowl of hot water to warm the sugar and gum tragacanth, and dissolve the dispersed gelatine by standing the container in hot water.

The history of the wedding cake

From our early civilizations the ritual of sharing food and drink has become part of our modern day wedding.

The early Romans called this sharing *confarreatio*, which means eating together. The Roman bride held 3 ears of wheat in her left hand whilst her right hand was held by the bridegroom. The wheat was symbolic of a life of plenty. At the conclusion of the ceremony the bridal party sat down together to partake of a simple cake, made from flour, salt and water.

Eventually it became the custom for the marriageable girls of the neighbourhood to assemble outside the church with measures of wheat, which they threw over the happy couple as they reappeared after the ceremony. Today this has been replaced by confetti or rice.

During the wheat throwing a scramble ensued among the guests to pick up the grains as they lay on the ground. It was considered a great compliment to the bride and groom to eat the wheat grains immediately.

Eventually the uncooked wheat kernels lost popularity, and a form of biscuit was crumbled over the couples' heads and the pieces scrambled for by the guests in the customary fashion. Today in the Scottish Highlands, an oatmeal cake is broken over the bride's head by the bridesmaid and the best man as she leaves the church, then portions are distributed to the guests.

During the reign of Elizabeth I, the biscuit developed into a rectangular bun or cake, made from flour, eggs, milk, sugar, currants and spices.

A further development took place when small cakes were made and coated with almond paste. Later these were created into one large cake, covered with hardened white sugar and decorated with symbolic cupids and doves, suggestive of matrimonial bliss.

Cake mixtures and recipes vary in different countries. In Italy the cake is usually a rich liqueur-drenched sponge, generously layered with cream, or a genoise cake. Sugar-coated almonds are souvenirs of the wedding; these are wrapped in tulle in uneven numbers and given to each guest.

France favours the towering *Croquembouche*, a magnificent structure of tiny choux profriteroles, based on a circle of shortbread or biscuit pastry, filled with cream and glazed with sugar toffee then decorated with spun sugar.

Norway has its special pyramid cake of almonds called *Kranodkake* which has been served at weddings for hundreds of years. This cake is broken after the toast to the bride and groom and is never cut with a knife.

The Danish cake also takes the form of a small tower of almond paste rings baked in the oven. Small figurines of the bride and groom top its pinnacle, surrounded by tiny Danish flags. Each almond paste ring is decorated with irregular lines of royal icing piped to form an interesting pattern. Small gifts for luck and tiny crackers surround the base of the tower.

In the Argentine the middle and lower classes serve sponge or genoise cakes decorated with almond paste and fondant. The more affluent people prefer a pudding-like fruit cake, decorated in a traditional manner.

In America the cake may be a rich genoise, or an angel food cake, ornately decorated with a smooth butter cream or frosting. Today many wedding cakes are of the rich fruit cake mixture, covered with almond paste and fondant and decorated more delicately.

Australia, England and South Africa all favour the rich fruit cake base with its almond paste and fondant cover. The cake is the centrepiece for the bridal table or it may be set on a special table of its own for all to admire.

Each country contributes its own influence as to the decorating of this very special cake. Originally the art of decorating cakes was dominated by male pastrycooks and bakers. It was not long before women, many of whom were housewives, developed their own techniques in the moulding of sugar paste flowers and leaves and showed their skill in the dainty piping of lace and embroidery. These attributes have earned them worldwide acclaim.

In Australia, almost every special occasion is celebrated with a decorated cake.

USEFUL HINTS

1. Where fondant or modelling paste has dried and hardened, it may be reconstituted by placing in a microwave oven for approximately 14 seconds, on medium-high. It should then be hand-kneaded until smooth and pliable.
2. An interesting-textured surface may be produced on modelling paste or fondant plaques by rolling a patterned plastic hair roller in several directions.
3. *Do not* allow gelatine to boil, as this impairs its gelling ability in a recipe, and pliability suffers as a result.
4. A modelling paste cone or flower centre for arum lilies, anthuriums, daisies and other similar flowers, appears more realistic when dampened, then rolled into semolina, polenta or fine gelatine, to produce a natural pollen effect.
5. Piping is frequently accompanied by interruptions of sufficient length to allow the royal icing to dry in the tube. To offset this, take a suitable plastic box with a lid. Line the base of the box with a piece of dampened sponge foam, cut a few holes in the lid approximately 5 cm in diameter and stand the bag erect in the hole with the point of the tube resting on the dampened foam.
6. Multi-coloured royal icing may be produced from an individual piping bag by firstly striping the inside of it with the desired paste colours applied with a paintbrush or bamboo saté stick, before being filled with royal icing. Liquid food colouring may also be applied in this way, but use it sparingly, so that it doesn't soften the overall consistency of the icing.
7. To keep your workbench or table neat and tidy, tape a plastic bag along the bench edge under the work board or plastic place mat. As the off-cuts accumulate from flower making etc., just brush them directly into the bag, leaving the work space clean.
8. Waxed paper is a well established medium on which to produce free standing pipework, however, it is necessary to have strong, high quality paper to avoid breakage when it is being released. Suitable quality is not always available and, as an alternative, "freezer go-between sheets" are recommended.
9. When incorporating strong colours such as red, green, black or violet, place the fondant or modelling paste inside a plastic bag. Make a small hole in the paste and add the colour, pinch the hole together and tightly tag the bag, leaving a suitable space inside to allow movement. Knead well from the outside of the plastic bag until the colour is evenly distributed throughout the mixture. Result — clean, unstained hands.
10. To make fine cotton stamens, draw a length of cotton thread through a piece of beeswax to stiffen, then cut the lengths as required to suit the various flowers.
11. Natural corn silk surrounding corn cobs also produces fine natural centres for flowers. Remove the corn silk and place on a piece of kitchen paper. Microwave on high for approximately 30 seconds or until the moisture dries from the silk. Allow to cool, then store it in a plastic bag in the refrigerator until required. Cut the lengths as required for the flowers.
12. To avoid inserting wires into a cake when attaching sprays, use a small dome of fondant and arrange the wired sprays and flowers into it. This eliminates the necessity to "poke" wires into the cake. It also allows the arrangement to be removed safely before the cake is cut.

GLOSSARY OF TERMS

Anger tool

A tapered stick, may be wood, metal or plastic, which is used for hollowing out a cone, or fluting edges.

Ball tools

Round balls varying in sizes from small to large, attached to a handle and used in softening the edges of petals and leaves.

Cake dividers

An ornamental structure, usually perspex, used to support and divide tiered cakes as an alternative to pillars.

Cleats

Wooden runners attached to the base board of the cake for support and to raise the board for ease in lifting the cake.

Cupping or hollowing

Hollowing small balls of sugar paste by inserting a tapered tool or the handle of a small paintbrush into the paste to produce a cup or cone shape.

Floodwork

A means by which a picture, scene or motif may be applied to a cake or plaque with royal icing, broken down with water or egg white until the consistency resembles a thick syrup.

Florist's tape

Stemtex or *Parafilm*, a stretch tape used for covering the wire that forms the stems of sugar flowers or leaves, singularly or as sprays.

Flower and leaf cutters

Sharp-edged metal or plastic reproductions of flower petal or leaf shapes, used for moulded flowers.

Flower marker

Also known as an umbrella tool, evenly marks petals.

Filler Flowers

Small paste flowers suitable to tuck between gaps left in floral arrangements or sprays.

Flower paste

A sugar paste, similar in texture to a fondant. It may be finely rolled and smoothed with the fingertips to produce flowers, petals and leaves. It is quick-drying and when it hardens it holds its shape indefinitely.

Flower stick tool

A pointed, semi-pointed or rounded object, inserted to open the throat of a moulded flower. It may also be used for fluting edges.

Glaze

A mixture of gelatine, water and glucose, used to produce a shine or waxed look to moulded flowers and leaves.

Gum/glue

A sticky edible substance made from gum arabic powder and water. The word "Glue" mentioned in this book refers to edible sticking substances such as water, egg white, gum arabic solution, or sticky gum sugar paste.

Log shape

Cylindrical or sausage-shaped piece of sugar paste or fondant.

Modelling paste

See flower paste.

Packing a cake

This means to fill any fruit holes, paper creases or other indentations with pieces of almond or marzipan paste or fondant. It is pressed well into the cavity with the blade of a knife or spatula to smooth it level with the cake, prior to covering.

Pillars

Supports between the tiers of cakes. These may be plastic, perspex or sugar paste.

Piping

The means whereby royal icing is forced through specific tubes attached or inserted into a piping bag and regulated by controlled hand pressure.

Run-in sugar

See Floodwork.

Scalpel

A sharp cutting implement with a short blade.

Smoothers

Trowel-like implements made from very smooth wood, plastic or perspex and used to smooth over the applied cake covering.

Smoothing the edge

Smoothing the edge or softening the cut edge of moulded flowers, leaves or pattern pieces by softly pressing the edge between the cushion of the thumb and index fingers or smoothing with a ball tool.

Snails trail

A small fine beading of royal icing.

Sugar paste

Equal quantities fondant and modelling paste.

Teardrop

See snails trail.

Template

A paper or cardboard pattern, used as a marker to transfer a design accurately onto or around a cake.

PATTERNS & TEMPLATES

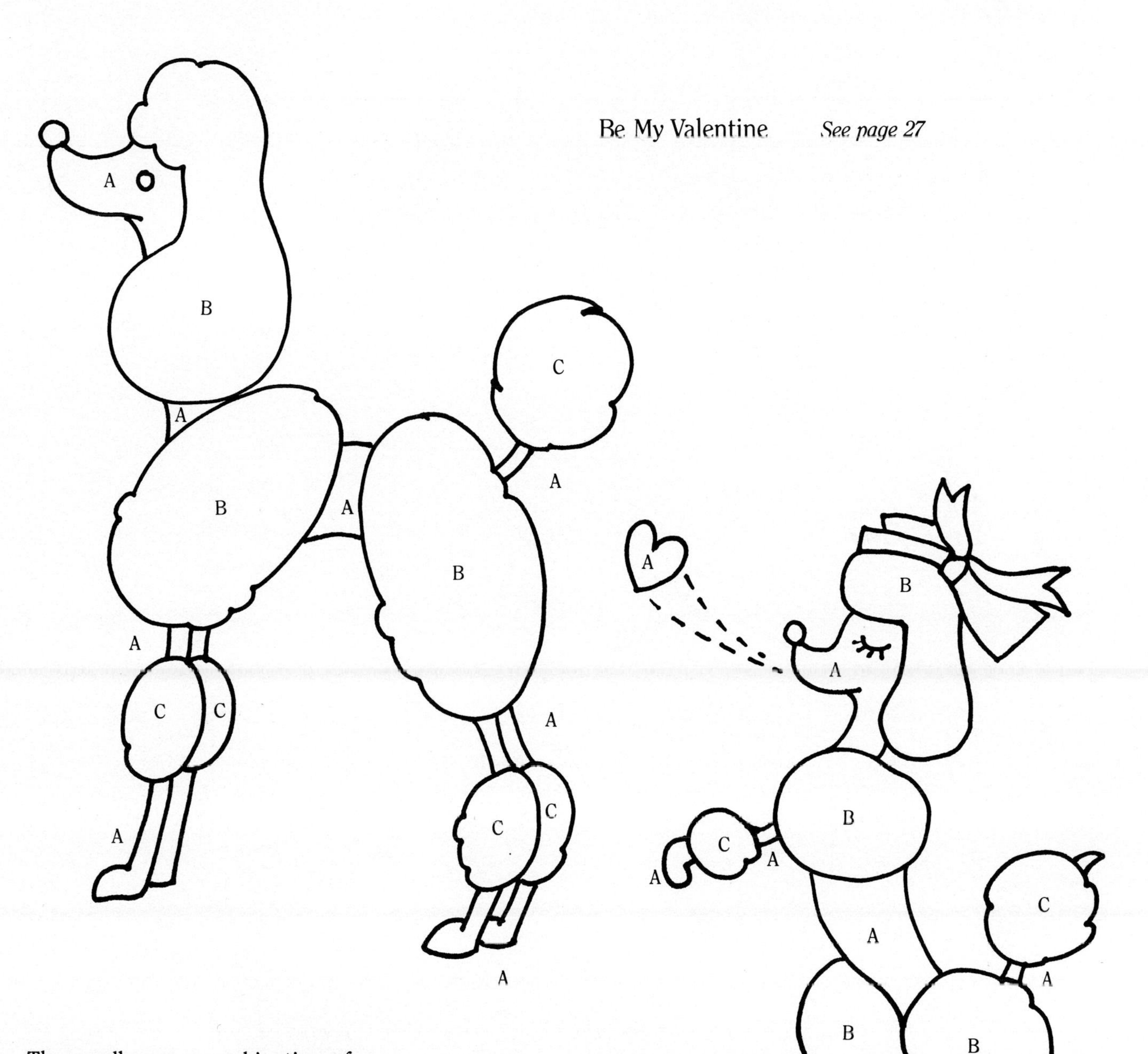

Be My Valentine *See page 27*

The poodles are a combination of flood work (run in sugar) and small and large piped stars.

Key: A Flood work
B No. 8 star tube
C No. 5 star tube

Both B and C use semi-firm peak consistency Royal icing.

All outlines are piped with No. 0 tube using soft peak consistency Royal icing.

Bluebird on My Finger *See page 32*

The Busy Squirrels

Sugar and Spice *See page 32*

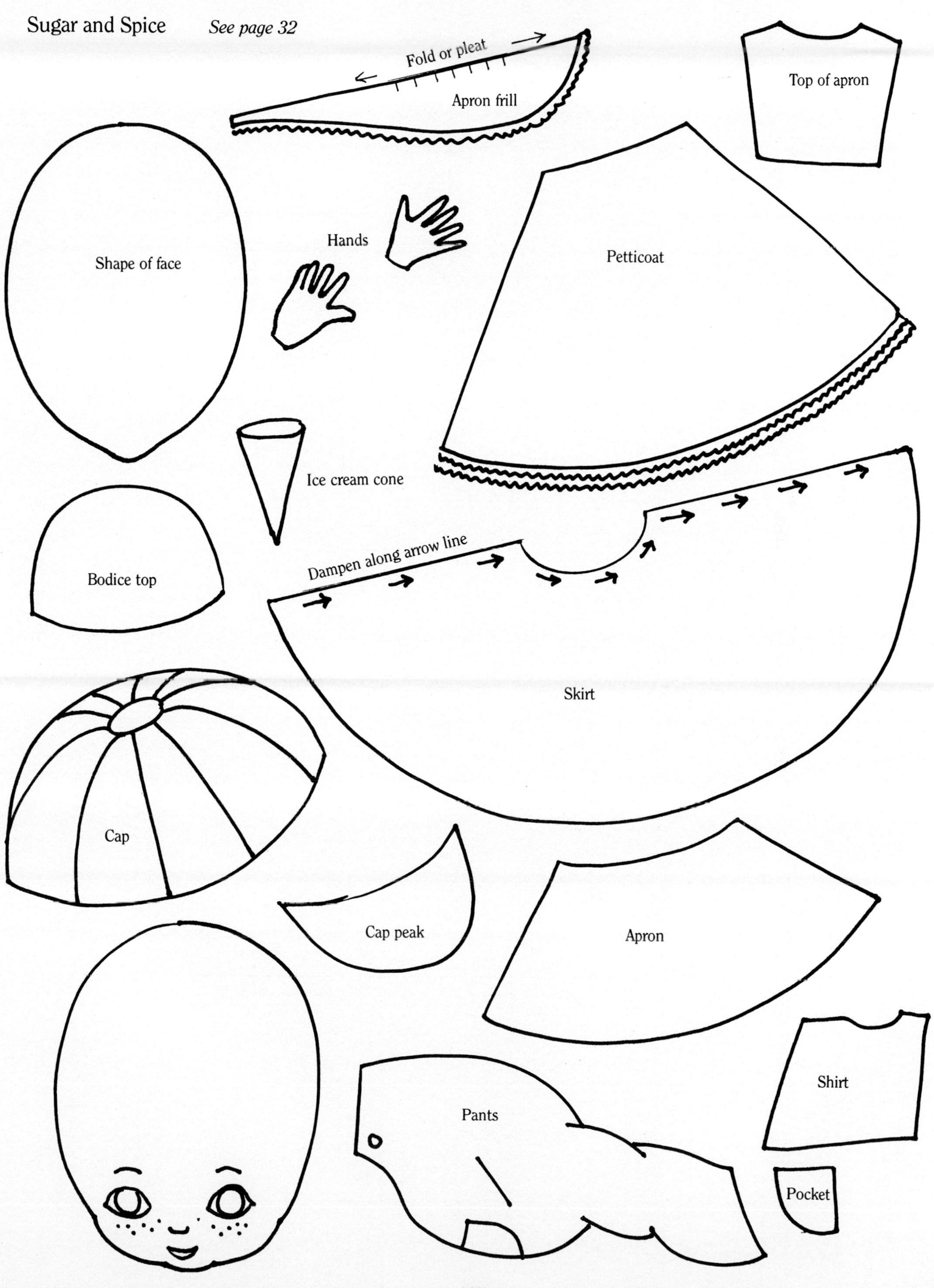

Someone's Halo is Slipping *See page 111*

Dotted lines represent lightly packed areas necessary to gain the body contour shape beneath the top sugar paste overlay.

Arm

Sleeve

Springtime is Funtime *See page 32*

Christmas Carol Angel

Sectioning a Royal Collar

See pages 36 and 37

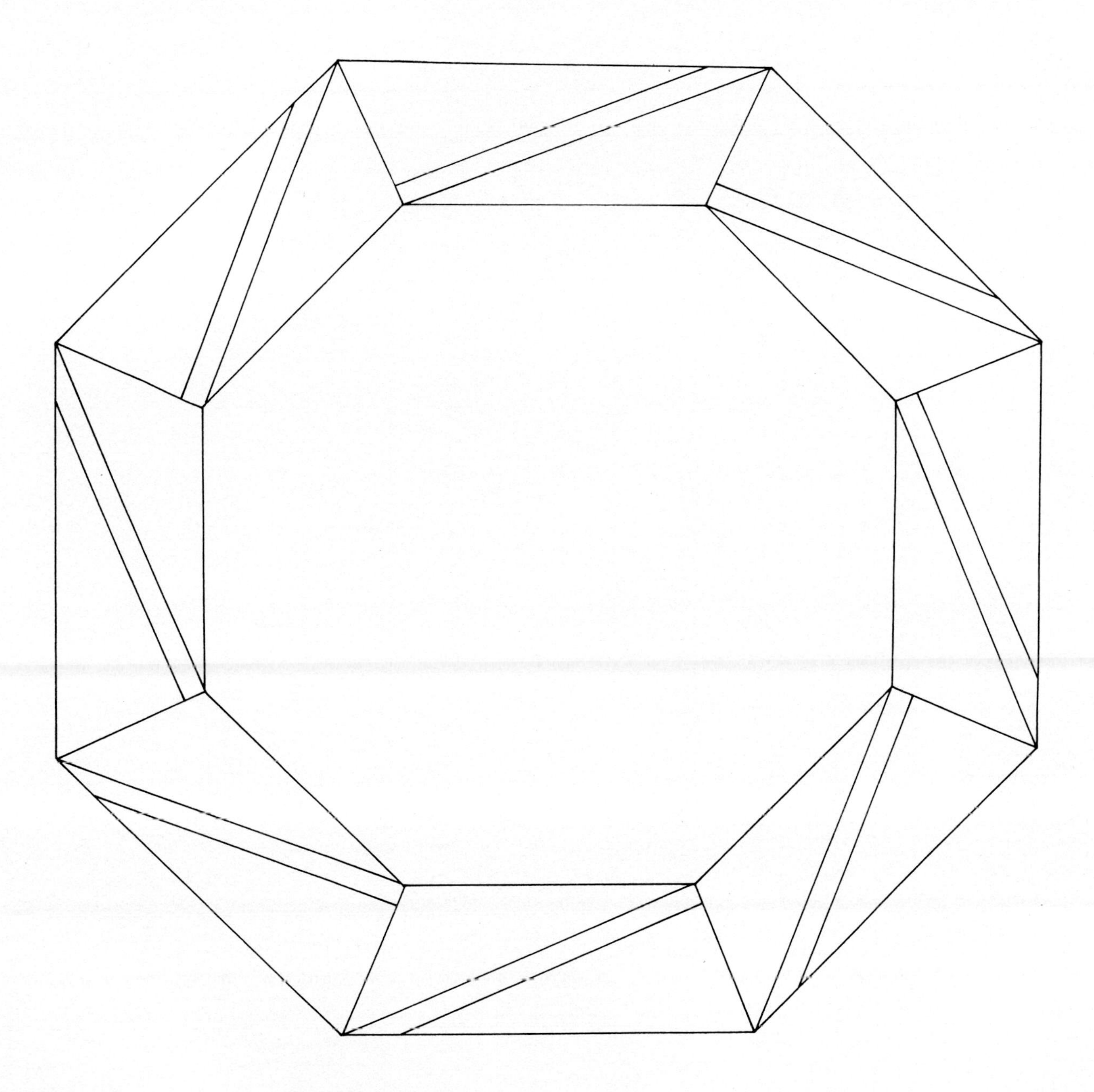

Pattern for Happy Birthday *card on page 6.*

Patchwork appliqué design *See page 51*

Figures refer to the order of execution.

Bibs with the Flounce *See page 102*

Moulded figures *See page 54*

Patterns for man's clothing

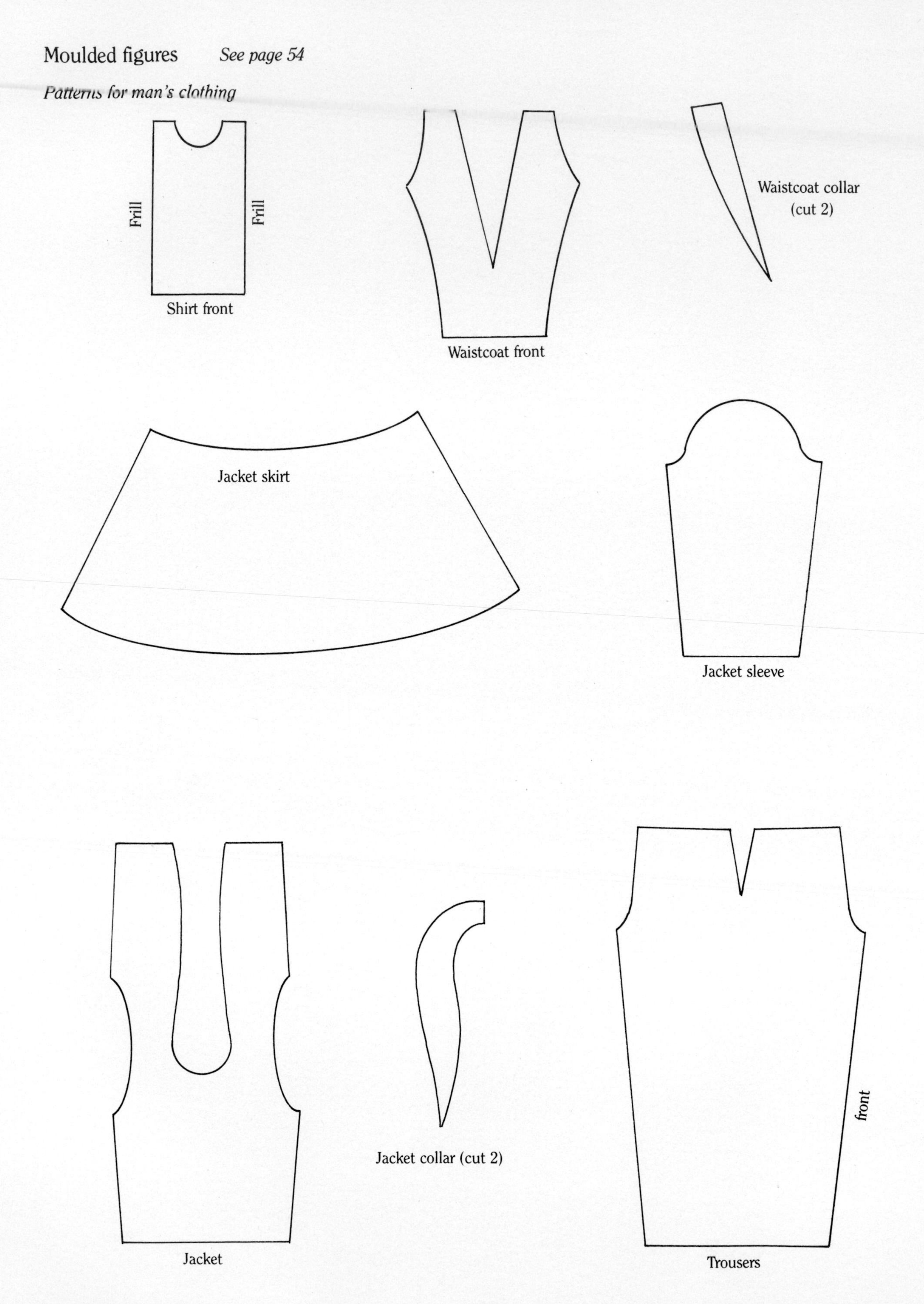